ENDORSEMENTS

"*Driven By Prayer* is an exceptional read for believers seeking the power of prayer. Bernie skillfully clarifies its complexities, offering revelation and insights. Get ready for real results and a deeper connection with Jesus. This book is a must in every Christian's library. I firmly believe it's timeless truth will change your life."

PASTOR CHRIS LINDBERG, Life Fellowship Church

"In an increasingly prayerless world, Bernie's latest book, *Driven By Prayer*, lays the foundation for all Christians to lean into the discipline of an active prayer life. Whether you've been a Christian for a day or all your days, this is a book worth reading. Bernie's heart for the world shines through and demonstrates the transformative power of prayer in all our lives."

PASTOR BENNY PEREZ, ChurchLV

"Bernie Moore embodies a life of prayer and faith. Leading evangelical crusades in some of the most remote, most forgotten places in the world requires it! I've had the privilege of traveling with him and seeing him boldly proclaim God's love, faithfulness, and power to literally over 100 thousand people in just one of these missionary journeys. When you meet someone whose very life is the proof of their message, (the walk is not only in keeping with the talk, the walk EXCEEDS the talk) the wise thing to do is lean in and absorb every word. In *Driven By Prayer* Bernie guides the reader step by step, through the Bible, into a new and vibrant life of prayer. I am honored and privileged to call him my friend."

PASTOR LAFE ANGELL, Lead Pastor, Grace Point Family Church.
Speaker and Author

"Prayer is not a gift man offers to God. It is a gift God offered to man. Prayer is powerful, intimate, necessary, and simple. This book is an invitation to find a refreshed place in prayer."

PASTOR EDDIE WOODS, City Point Church

"You don't gather nations and impact 100,000's of souls without an exceptional relationship with Jesus. Bernie Moore has lived this message before our eyes and is now kind enough to give us the map that led him to his treasure. This book will provoke you to go deeper with God."

MARK FRANCEY, Founding Pastor
Oceans Church, Orange County, California

"I have known Bernie for over 25 years and have seen his passion for God and the call on his life drive him to places all over the world for Jesus' name sake. This book is a 'backstage pass,' to the furnace of prayer and purpose Bernie has walked in for decades. This isn't information, it is an impartation!"

JASON ROBINSON, Senior Pastor
Church of The King, Katy, Texas

DRIVEN BY PRAYER

DRIVEN BY PRAYER

Discover the One Who Never Changes

Bernie Moore

Carpenter's Son Publishing

Driven by Prayer
Discover the One Who Never Changes

A Publication of Bernie Moore Ministries

Published by Carpenter's Son Publishing, Franklin, Tennessee
www.carpenterssonpublishing.com

Interior Design by Suzanne Lawing

Printed in the United States of America

ISBN: 978-1-956370-23-2 (print)

ACKNOWLEDGEMENTS

I would first like to thank my Lord and Savior—my Jesus, who's wrapped me in His everlasting love! He's clothed me in unspeakable mercy, grace and forgiveness. I want to thank my beautiful wife who introduced me to my loving Savior. Thank you for your extreme love and your patience with me over the last 31 years of being together and nearly 25 years being married. You are the greatest gift Heaven has bestowed upon me. Thank you for our three beautiful children, Caitlyn, Claire and Caleb. You guys are my treasures. I love you so much.

Foreword

In a world that often demands action, speed, and results, it's easy to overlook the quiet, transformative power of prayer. Yet, throughout history, prayer has been the steadfast companion of those who sought not just to live, but to live with purpose. *Driven by Prayer* is a testament to that sacred journey—a journey where faith meets action, and where the whispers of the soul are amplified through divine guidance.

This book is not just a collection of thoughts, life stories and scriptures but a heartfelt exploration of how prayer can and should drive every aspect of our lives. *Driven By Prayer* delves into the deep, glorious and sometimes mysterious, connection between our spiritual practices of communioning with our Heavenly Father and the tangible outcomes we seek in this temporary world. Whether you are a seasoned believer or someone searching for deeper meaning, this book offers a beautiful well thought out roadmap to navigate life's challenges with grace, resilience, and unshakable faith.

I've known Bernie Moore for almost 25 years and I know him to be a man devoted to prayer. His passion to know the Lord is truly contagious. But as he clearly reveals in this book, it all begins with prayer. So, as you turn these pages, you'll discover that prayer is not a passive retreat but a dynamic force that propels us forward, aligning our hearts with God's. The stories, insights, and reflections within will inspire you to embrace prayer not just as a ritual, but as a driving force that shapes your destiny.

May this book ignite in you a renewed passion for prayer and lead you to discover the extraordinary power it holds to transform your life.

—Pastor Benny Perez

Contents

Introduction

"Is it worth it? I'm not sure, to be honest." I slowly open my eyes only to realize it's still dark. It's not only cold but I'm exhausted, and if I'm being honest I really don't feel like getting out of bed. As the minutes tick on, I continue negotiating in my head, trying hard to devise every excuse I possibly can, telling myself I could really use one more hour of sleep. After all, lately life has been coming at me like a fury: finances, family, marriage, friends, ministry, travel, health, and the list goes on. It seems as though I can't catch a break. Everyone needs something from me, and yet, who can I turn to for solace and comfort? Then, a soft, gentle voice whispers a familiar Scripture: "The spirit is indeed willing, but the flesh is weak." (Matthew 26:41) Knowing what I have to do, I talk myself out of bed. First, coffee! Next, my home office, where I sit in the stillness of the early morning. I sometimes begin quietly in my mind and softly aloud, thanking God for the many blessings He's bestowed upon me. Even in moments of trials, there are always things to be thankful for; I don't have to look very far. The seconds quickly turn into minutes; these days, those minutes are hours, but it all started with making a simple decision, deciding to swing my legs out of bed and get up.

With the daily battles and struggles we all face, some may even seem herculean, I believe the first action of every day must, without question, be prayer! It is the most important action of our entire day.

We must be Driven By Prayer! Setting our affections on the Lord through prayer, instantly places us in God's holy presence and sets us up to handle any and all challenges that may come our way. For me, this has become a non-negotiable. I have to spend time with Jesus! My heart yearns for Him.

Several years after starting Bernie Moore Ministries International, our global evangelism ministry, I found myself in an extended time of prayer one morning. We'd been conducting our global Jesus Festivals for several years when I realized that we saw people coming to Jesus for an average ministry cost of one dollar, sometimes even less, per soul. Of course, this was shocking, in a good way! My sincere goal was always to make every dollar stretch as far as possible to reach as many people as possible. So, when I realized that for every dollar a donor gave, a soul was being saved, I paused with great excitement. Unfortunately, the excitement didn't last long. The joy I had felt quickly turned into a holy frustration.

I began to think to myself, "This is just simple math. Based on these numbers, if we had one million dollars, we could win one million souls for the Lord." Again, I paused, thinking, how could I only now be realizing this? Honestly, that particular morning while in prayer, my disappointment grew. This really bothered me. I cried out in prayer, saying, "Lord, please give us one million dollars, and we will reach and win one million souls. Every penny would go toward our Jesus Festivals all over Africa, Asia, and the rest of the world!" As moments passed, I became more passionate about my pleas to the Lord, continuing to ask, basically begging Him to send us the funds so that we could turn them into one million lost, hurting, and broken souls won to Jesus. After several minutes of lingering in prayer over this, I finally quieted down. (My wife would say that's the first miracle.) I must admit, I became a bit emotional. Tears streamed down my face. As I sat in silence, still thinking we needed a million dollars to reach a million souls, the Lord softly replied in the stillness of the moment and said, *"Bernie, you don't have a million-dollar prayer life!"* It was there in that very moment that I realized my life was not consumed with prayer - it was not *"Driven By Prayer!"*

I remember what the Lord spoke to me years ago when He said, *"Bernie, if you want to go where you've never gone so that you can see what you've never seen and do what you've never done, then you must be willing to pay a price you've never paid!"*

Jesus modeled a faithful life of prayer for us. The disciples could've asked Him many questions such as, "Could you please teach us how to sustain or even grow this great ministry You've started?" or, maybe, "Teach us how to plant churches or birth new ministries so we can reach more people" or maybe "Teach us how to grow our partner base so we can raise more support to bring this glorious Gospel around the world," they could've gone on and asked, "Can you please teach us how to preach effectively like You do," or, even, "Teach us how to perform miracles and cast out demons" or maybe "Teach us how to disciple new believers and handle religious and community leaders." I'm sure these questions would've all been good and well-intended. Surely, we would've understood why they'd asked such things, but none of these questions left their lips. The only question that truly plagued them was, **"Lord, teach us to pray!"** They saw their Lord and Savior model this so well that they wanted His prayer life more than anything else. Again, "Lord, teach us to pray!" They began to learn the vital importance of being Driven By Prayer. Charles Spurgeon wrote, "Groanings that cannot be uttered are often prayers that cannot be refused." May we all be driven by a spirit of prayer!

What did Jesus say about John the Baptist? As a man who lived a life devoted to prayer, alone in the wilderness, he passionately and unapologetically pursued God with his entire being. He was clothed in camel's hair, girded with a leather belt (not Gucci), and he didn't really give two hoots about whether anyone liked him or approved of his life. He regularly feasted on a diet of locusts and wild honey. And yet, Jesus said of this man, "There has been none born of women greater than John the Baptist." Even Herod, a heathen king who feared no one, actually feared John the Baptist. Mark writes in chapter 6, verse

20, "Herod feared John for he knew he was a just and holy man and he protected him. Herod enjoyed listening to John." It's easy to see that Herod knew there was something very unique about John; he had something that Herod wanted. Despite the king having accumulated worldly wealth, great influence, and numerous accolades, nothing seemed to satisfy him. Although John didn't possess the worldly achievements that Herod had, Herod knew and truly recognized that what John possessed was far greater than all he had attained. John's life was not his own. He fully belonged to God. What John possessed couldn't be bought with money or achieved by artificial, earthly means. John had a deep, pure, genuine, and holy relationship with his Heavenly Father. That relationship was only attained through a life Driven By Prayer!

My heart for this book is that you would become so passionate about prayer that it would drive your every waking moment and that you would realize communing with the Father is what we were all created to do. He longs to speak with you and for you to long for Him, too! Through this divine Spirit, you'll realize prayer propels us forward and gives life to every dream we have. As oxygen gives life to our lungs and blood gives life to the body, prayer gives life to our spirit and connects us right to the heart of the Father. May the words written on the pages of this book greatly impact you and challenge you to live a life Driven By Prayer.

Chapter One

The God Who Sees Me

You are one of eight billion people wandering this planet. That number alone is enough to make anyone feel insignificant. Have you ever thought, "I wonder if anyone even notices me? Am I alone? Does anyone care? What about God? Does He even listen when I speak? Forget about listening to me; does He even see me?" "Then she called the name of the Lord who spoke to her, 'You are a God who sees'; for she said, 'Have I even remained alive here after seeing Him?'" (Genesis 16:13 NASB).

God saw Hagar. Abraham and Sarai had taken God's promise of bearing children into their own hands, making a real mess of things. Hagar was a victim of convenience, an unfortunate party to a misuse of God's Word. Sarai told Abraham to sleep with her maidservant, leading to trouble for Hagar. Sarai was cruel to her, so cruel she ran away into the desert. Rejected, lost, alone, and broken, her life was now clothed in despair. This is where God met her. She was at the end of her rope when she finally decided to call out to God, and boy, did He answer.

"And the Angel of the Lord said to her: 'Behold, you are with child, And you shall bear a son'" (Genesis 16:11 NKJV). Then Hagar called the name of the Lord who spoke to her, "You-Are-the-God-Who-Sees," but according to the Hebrew word "rō-'î," it means, "a God of seeing." Therefore, El Roi means "The God who sees me."

El Roi—He is the God of compassion. He sees. He knows. God sees and knows you. You don't have any heartache, pain, trouble, or rejection that God doesn't know about. First Peter 3:12 reminds us that God's eye is on each of us. "For the eyes of the Lord are on the righteous, And his ears are open to their prayers" (NKJV).

God sees: "'Can anyone hide himself in secret places, So I shall not see him?' says the Lord; 'Do I not fill heaven and earth?' says the Lord" (Jeremiah 23:24 NKJV).

God hears: "Now this is the confidence that we have in Him, that if we ask anything according to His will, He hears us" (1 John 5:14 NKJV).

God speaks: "And it came to pass, when Moses entered the tabernacle, that the pillar of cloud descended and stood at the door of the tabernacle, and the Lord talked with Moses" (Exodus 33:9 NKJV).

God is With Us—God Sees Us

You must understand that God sees you and knows you intimately. He knows everything about you and loves you with a ferocious kind of love. He is very well acquainted with the desires hidden in the depths of your heart. He knows very well the things that trouble you. Still, wanting to pull a page from Adam and Eve's playbook is human nature, to run and hide because we feel the Lord doesn't understand. There's no need to call out to Him, we think; He won't answer anyway. We must know that God will not only answer but will always provide a way for us that seems impossible. Look no further than our old friend Moses.

Most of us are familiar with the story of Moses and the burning bush. In Exodus, Moses was a shepherd, tending to sheep when God appeared to him as a bush on fire. God called Moses to be His mouthpiece, but His speech stands out to me most: "And the Lord said: 'I have surely seen the oppression of My people who are in Egypt, and have heard their cry because of their taskmasters, for I know their sorrows. So I have come down to deliver them out of the hand of the Egyptians, and to bring them up from that land to a good and large land, to a land flowing with milk and honey, to the place of the Canaanites and the Hittites and the Amorites and the Perizzites and the Hivites and the Jebusites. Now therefore, behold, the cry of the children of Israel has come to Me, and I have also seen the oppression with which the Egyptians oppress them. Come now, therefore, and I will send you to Pharaoh that you may bring My people, the children of Israel, out of Egypt'" (Exodus 3:7-10 NKJV). When God hears the cries of His children, He doesn't just appear to us with nice words. He is a God of action.

God cares for humanity. When we cry out, He will answer. Although we may sometimes feel like God has forsaken us due to our trials and tribulations, we must realize that God is there and on our side. He will make a way where there is no way. The Israelites saw this with their own eyes when God parted the Red Sea before them.

GOD CARES FOR HUMANITY. WHEN WE CRY OUT, HE WILL ANSWER. ALTHOUGH WE MAY SOMETIMES FEEL LIKE GOD HAS FORSAKEN US DUE TO OUR TRIALS AND TRIBULATIONS, WE MUST REALIZE THAT GOD IS THERE AND ON OUR SIDE. HE WILL MAKE A WAY WHERE THERE IS NO WAY. THE ISRAELITES SAW THIS WITH THEIR OWN EYES WHEN GOD PARTED THE RED SEA BEFORE THEM.

Though people have true feelings, these feelings do not always tell the truth. Only God's Word is the truth, whether we feel it or not. When we feel like God is not near, we must remember He has said, "The Lord is near to all who call upon Him, To all who call upon Him in truth." (Psalm 145:18 NKJV). Reading the

Bible and spending time in prayer will always remind us how much God cares for us, and His words are always encouraging. When we're walking through moments or seasons of great struggle, we naturally question if the Lord is even with us. During these times of confusion or despair, we hide and keep it all in or refrain from prayer because we feel abandoned, isolated, and alone. Isaiah battled these same thoughts. God promises us that He is not only with us, but He is also holding our hand.

> PRAYER IS THE GATEWAY THROUGH WHICH GOD SEES YOU AND DEMONSTRATES HIS ATTENTION AND CONCERN.

"For I, the Lord your God, will hold your right hand, Saying to you, 'Fear not, I will help you.'" (Isaiah 41:13 NKJV).

"When you pass through the waters, I will be with you; And through the rivers, they shall not overflow you. When you walk through the fire, you shall not be burned, Nor shall the flame scorch you." (Isaiah 43:2 NKJV).

When God sees you, your prayers bring your heart into immediate contact with the wellspring of life, the living God, and strengthen the soul, mind, will, and emotion, as your whole being is empowered by God's presence. Prayer is the gateway through which God sees you and demonstrates His attention and concern. When you can feel His presence, prayer becomes very intimate, a whispering of the soul with God.

God Sees You

Have you ever felt forgotten by someone you love? If so, you're not alone. Consider David, who became the greatest king Israel has ever known and through whose lineage Jesus was born into the world. It wasn't always this way; originally, David was a nobody, herding sheep in the field. His only responsibility was looking after his father's flock, while it seemed like other people had greater callings. While David watched everyone close to him seemingly handling important responsibilities, he woke up every day shoveling you-know-what and probably had the mindset of inferiority. He must have asked himself, "Why am I the only one out here alone just watching sheep eat? Why do I have to risk my life for them? Everyone else gets to go fight in battles, and I'm the one out here alone with stinky, smelly, dumb sheep." To add insult to injury, one day, Samuel, the greatest prophet of Israel, decided to visit David's little obscure town of Bethlehem. He knocked on the door of David's father Jesse's home and told him that God had sent him to anoint one of his sons as the next king. Jesse lined up his seven older sons, leaving David in the wilderness, not even thinking he could be the one God wanted. BUT GOD.

David was the one God had in mind. Like he did with David, God knows your worth when other people don't see your value. It was during his times of loneliness and isolation that David had learned to fight. He'd learned to defend the helpless sheep against the lions' ferocious roars and the bears' deep growls. Scripture says he even killed these animals with his own bare hands!

During a battle against the Philistines, the Israeli army came to a complete standstill. As a man named Goliath of Gath hurled some of the most vile insults possible against the Lord and His people, it was then that this obscure, lonely, forgotten shepherd boy came to bring his brothers and their friends some cheese and crackers. He heard the repeated hellacious insults that spewed from this giant named Goliath.

To David's amazement, the entire army of Israel was frozen. These great warriors cowered in fear because of one man's obnoxiousness. David looked around, confused, because these were the same guys he had once revered. Finally, after several moments of silence, David spoke up and said to Saul, the king, "I will go and fight this barbarian." And he continued, "The Lord, who delivered me from the paw of the lion and from the paw of the bear, He will deliver me from the hand of this Philistine" (1 Samuel 17:34-37 NKJV).

David's greatest weapon was not five smooth stones; his greatest weapon was the time he had spent in isolation learning how to trust in the Lord so that when the bear and the lion came to attack, that power rose within him, making him victorious over the beasts. This is what prayer does to us; it clothes us with confidence. It ignites a spirit of courage in us which will equip us and prepare us for life's challenges. This confidence led a young boy to victory with a child's weapon. God can do much with very little. The greatest thing we possess as believers is the gift of prayer, for God will not reject a surrendered heart.

God Sees Elijah on Mount Sinai

It doesn't matter if you are an exalted man or woman of God or if you feel like you are hiding in the cracks and crevices of life. God sees you. You are always on His mind.

Elijah walked so closely with God that He sent a chariot of fire down to collect him at the end of his life. Like all of us, Elijah battled the war of thoughts. In 1 Kings 18, in the midst of a great victory where Elijah singlehandedly defeated 450 prophets of Baal armed with nothing more than the gift of prayer from his God, he was threatened by a woman named Jezebel who put a bounty on his head. He was so overwhelmed with fear that the spirit of Forrest Gump jumped on him, and he went on the run for days. Finally, he wore himself down and wound up near a creek, overwhelmed with so much discouragement and despair that he literally prayed that he might die. (Thankfully, God didn't answer his prayer. Sometimes, there is sweet blessing in unanswered prayers.) Instead, God sent His angel to comfort him and feed him and give him water. (I wonder if God gave him a #1 from Chick-fil-A.) He got up to eat and lay back down again. Then, the angel came back a second time! Thank God that He didn't give up on Elijah and that He doesn't give up on us, either. God is a God who never gives up. This time, the angel said, "Arise, the journey is too great for you." God has great plans for you, too. The things planned for you are so great that you could never accomplish them without Him. God is saying to you, the reader, right now that He has great plans for you, and it's time to arise and move forward on those plans with His help! C'mon, somebody!

Elijah began to pray. He did the very thing God wants all of us to do, even though he was tired and weary. Even though he was confused and on the run, he prayed. He poured his heart out to the Lord. And then he said, "Lord, I have been very zealous, but I'm the only one left with this sort of passion and zeal, and everyone seeks to take my life." God responded, "You're not alone. I'm with you. And 7,000 others haven't bowed their knees to Baal."

You may feel the same way Elijah felt. Isolated, alone, as if no one can relate or understand what you're going through. Nobody has sympathy for your situation, and because of it, like Elijah tried to do, you want to throw your hands in the air and just give up. But also, like Elijah, I want to encourage you to pause and pray even as you read these words right now. Ask the Holy Spirit to reveal Himself and let you know the plans He has right now for you in this season and situation of life. God is faithful, and God is good. God promises to answer the cry of your heart and respond when you call.

The Lord taught Elijah a very valuable lesson. The Scripture says He took Elijah up on the side of the mountain, and a great and strong wind tore into the mountains and broke it up into large pieces of rock that fell away, but the Lord said He was not in the wind. Next was an earthquake; again, God wasn't in it. Finally, a fire burned greatly, but God was not there, either. After these three expressions of power, the Scripture says there was a still, small voice—a whisper. God was in the whisper. "What are you doing here, Elijah?" said the quiet voice.

God doesn't need to move supernaturally with wind, earthquakes, rain, or any other expression of outward power. God desires to whisper to us in prayer. When we take time to get with God, we hear His beautiful voice.

Why did God whisper? God doesn't need to move supernaturally with wind, earthquakes, rain, or any other expression of outward power. God desires to whisper to us in prayer. When we take time to get with God, we hear His beautiful voice. The most important thing is that we recognize that God sees us. This should be the main ingredient of our lives. God is in the whisper, in the secret place, waiting for us to come away and pray. He's waiting for us to get away from the distractions and chaos of life, and He's waiting for us to come to His feet. When we prioritize spending time with God, He will make it a priority to speak to us.

The God Who Hears

"Hear, O Lord, when I cry with my voice! Have mercy also upon me, and answer me" (Psalm 27:7 NKJV). Chaim Bentorah, a Hebrew scholar, wrote about the biblical perspective on Psalm 27:7, which shows that God wants us to ask when needed.

After expressing reasons to be fully confident in God's protection, David desperately pleaded with the Lord to answer his prayer. Perhaps he saw the enemy bearing down on him. David's eyes may have focused more on his enemy than on the Lord. He knew that he did not deserve an answer from the Lord. After all, he was a sinner like all of us. He simply appealed to the Lord to be gracious to him and to answer him.

Rather than contradicting the first six verses of this psalm, David's prayer here was a natural reaction. He knew he had no reason to fear—but that knowledge does not make human beings immune to anxiety. Psalm 27, then, is a mixture of prayer and self-reassurance. David expressed his need for God, stating his trust and weakness all at once. We see a father saying something similar in Mark 9:24, "Immediately the father of the child cried out and said, 'I believe; help my unbelief!'" (ESV).

"Hebrew is an emotional language. You cannot just look up a word in your Lexicon and say you now know what a word means in the original Hebrew. You must take this word for a walk, live with it, experience it, feel it, play with it, argue with it, and build a relationship with it before you understand it. You must never translate a word that has not been first translated into your heart."

As Chaim Bentorah continues, "Using the word shama in an imperative form shows the depth of anguish that David is experiencing. For him to cry out to God to listen to him, submit to his request, obey, and become one with 'his voice' shows David's desperation. If you have never felt abandoned by God, never felt like your words were flying up, but your thoughts were remaining below, you will not understand the true depth of this passage."

If you have had this experience or are even experiencing it now, you are in a good position to translate this verse with your heart and begin to understand the heart of David and what he was saying.

David was asking God to obey the cry of his voice. The word "cry" is "kara," which is a call to meet or assemble. The word for voice is "koli," making a sound, which has a paragoge, meaning to express different emphasis. In this case, it makes this not only a voice, but also a voice of anguish. "David is doing more than just asking God to listen; he begs that God become a part of his anguish."

Hebrews 4:15 is relevant: "For we do not have a high priest who cannot sympathize with our weakness but One who has been tempted in all things just as we are, yet without sin" (NASB). Jesus, as our high priest, understands our weaknesses, and David wanted God to be a part of his anguished voice, not just a lofty God who was far away. For David to use the word "shama" in an imperative form shows that God is willing and ready and wants to jump into the pit with us. All we have to do is what David did—ask.

The Names of God

Before moving forward with this chapter, "The God Who Sees Me," it is valuable for the reader to understand the actual name of God and not be confused. Throughout Scripture, God reveals Himself to us through His names. When we study the names revealed in the Bible, we will better understand who God is. The meanings behind God's names show the central personality and nature of the One who displays them.

In the Old Testament, "Yahweh" occurs 6,823 times. It appears more than any other name of God. We see "Yahweh" first in Genesis 4:2, and it is the promised name of God. This name, which by Jewish tradition is too holy to voice, is spelled "YHWH" without vowels. Two other words for God are used in the Old Testament, "Jehovah" and "Lord."

In Exodus 6:1, the verse is translated according to the translator's view of the original, since all three words appear in the Old Testament.

"And YHWH says to Moses, 'Now you see that which I do to Pharaoh, for with a strong hand he sends them away, indeed, with a strong hand he casts them out of his land'" (LSV).

"And JEHOVAH saith unto Moses, 'Now dost thou see that which I do to Pharaoh, for with a strong hand he doth send them away, yea, with a strong hand he doth cast them out of his land'" (YLT).

"Then the Lord said to Moses, 'Now you shall see what I will do to Pharaoh. For with a strong hand he will let them go, and with a strong hand he will drive them out of his land'" (NKJV).

When God Sees a Soul

Jesus went to the Mount of Olives. Early in the morning, He came again to the temple. Everyone came to Him, and He sat down and taught them. Picture this: Jesus is doing His usual teaching thing, surrounded by a bunch of folks soaking up His wisdom. He's got the crowd's attention, but then the Pharisees bring a woman caught in adultery to Him, trying to throw her under the sinners' bus right in the middle of Jesus' teaching.

According to the law, getting caught in adultery meant you'd be on the fast track to getting stoned. The Pharisees looked at Jesus, basically saying, "What's your take on this?" They were totally missing the point because all they saw was another sinner, and they were convinced they were doing God's work.

Here's where it gets interesting. Instead of dropping some legal knowledge, Jesus began drawing in the dirt with His finger. The Pharisees were trying to trap Him, but Jesus shut them down. He stood up and said, "He that is without sin among you, let him first cast a stone at her." Everyone began to leave, from the older Pharisees to the younger ones, leaving Jesus alone with the accused woman. He asked her if anyone condemned her, and she realized her accusers were gone. Then Jesus said, "Neither do I condemn you: go, and sin no more."

While everyone else was focused on the outward sin, Jesus saw beyond that. He wasn't just aware of the accused soul; He saw through the accusers, too. It's like He was saying, "Only someone sinless can throw stones, and guess what? None of you qualify." Jesus is all about freeing our accused souls from judgment and telling us to turn away from sin.

This is a reminder that God's vision is well beyond ours. Humans can't see into each other's souls, but God can. As it says in Jeremiah, "I, the Lord, search the heart, I test the mind, To give to each person according to his ways, According to the results of his deeds" (Jeremiah 17:10 NASB).

When the disciples were replacing Judas in Acts 1:24, they looked to God for an answer and prayed, "Lord, you know everyone's heart. Show us which of these two you have chosen" (NIV). But this time, God let them choose.

Rest assured, God sees past the fake, the phony, the heartache, the pain, the failures, and the countless mistakes. He looks into the depths of your heart and sees a son or daughter, made righteous through the blood of His precious and holy Son, our Savior Jesus. It's here in this place, this secret place, that He longs for us to come away with Him and pray. "'For My thoughts are not your thoughts, Nor are your ways My ways,' says the Lord. 'For as the heavens are higher than the earth, So are My ways higher than your ways, And My thoughts than your thoughts'" (Isaiah 55:8-9 NKJV).

REST ASSURED, GOD SEES PAST THE FAKE, THE PHONY, THE HEARTACHE, THE PAIN, THE FAILURES, AND THE COUNTLESS MISTAKES. HE LOOKS INTO THE DEPTHS OF YOUR HEART AND SEES A SON OR DAUGHTER, MADE RIGHTEOUS THROUGH THE BLOOD OF HIS PRECIOUS AND HOLY SON, OUR SAVIOR JESUS.

Chapter Two

Faith—The Soulmate of Prayer

Faith and prayer go together like air and your lungs. You can't survive without either one. Hebrews 11:1 says, "Now faith is the substance of things hoped for, the evidence of things not seen" (NKJV).

In Mark 9, a father brought his demon-possessed son to be healed by Jesus' disciples, but they failed. At the end of his rope, moments away from giving up, the man asked Jesus to heal his son if he can. Jesus replied, "'If you can believe, all things are possible to him who believes.' Immediately, the child's father cried out and said with tears, 'Lord, I believe; help my unbelief!'" (Mark 9:23-24 NKJV).

Amid the father's vulnerability, he asked Jesus an honest question but one that was a little insulting. The boy's father was desperate; he pleaded with Jesus to have mercy on them and help… "IF YOU CAN." I have to believe there are not too many things that puzzled Jesus, but I do believe this question may have. Jesus must have thought, what kind of question is that? If I can? I believe the Lord, in one sense, was saying, do you know who it is you are speaking with? Do you know who I am? Have you heard what I've already done?

Most of us may be in the same position as this boy's father. We may not recognize the power that rests in the One whose holy ears catch prayers that leave our lips. It's very possible and highly probable that we do not realize the power He, to whom our feeble prayers are directed, possesses. There is simply NOTHING He cannot do. Jesus says that anything is possible for him who believes.

This word, "anything," literally means, "ANY THING." The only quality one must possess is a simple belief in Christ—not in man, not in church, and not in a pastor, but in Christ, the Author and Finisher of our faith. So, Jesus was puzzled. He turned the tables and said, the real question is, can you believe?

Jesus changed the question: It's not whether I can do it, but can YOU believe in Me? The father stood there, inches away from the only One who could help him, his face covered in tears of desperation, and he said a resounding, Yes! Lord, I believe. I really do believe. Then, there was a brief pause, and the father made one final request: Lord, if there's any unbelief, please help my unbelief. The father simply couldn't take seeing his son tormented daily by this demonic activity and witnessing the pain and turmoil he was in. To say he was desperate is an understatement. Lord, if there is any unbelief, help me. That was all Jesus needed to hear. That was the key that unlocked the door to the supernatural. The moment of vulnerability, honesty—if there are any seeds of unbelief, help me!

Later, the disciples came to Jesus puzzled and asked why they could not heal the boy. Amazingly, Jesus didn't rebuke them for coming to Him; instead, He rebuked them for being faithless! Faith is the oxygen to the soul; it's the fuel that gives fire to your prayers. Very rarely will you see your prayers have any effectiveness without them being mixed with faith, knowing that what you are praying for God will do!

Faith is the bedrock of our trust in the Lord! We can find ourselves in similar circumstances to the father in this story. We go to a friend, a pastor, a leader, or a mentor first, when, in reality, we, like the boy's father, could have saved a lot of time, trouble, and heartache if we had just gone to Jesus first.

Most of us have no concept of the power of the One to whom we are praying. We pray with the same attitude the father of the boy did; we say, "Jesus, if you can, please help me! Please heal me, please deliver me from this issue that's plagued me, save me, set me free, help me find my soulmate, lead me to a better job, touch my finances," and more. We approach Jesus with that same "if you can" mindset. A doubtful, unbelieving spirit plagues our prayers and causes them to be ineffective.

The other part of this story is that the father never gave up. When the disciples couldn't heal his son, he didn't get bitter but instead went to Jesus. The twelve people who were closest to Jesus and were supposed to mirror His life the most failed miserably, and this was why Jesus rebuked them in front of everyone. You see, Jesus does not like to be misrepresented. This is an offense to Him. So, He first rebuked the leaders, His best friends, and His closest confidants because they, who should have had the power to heal, simply did not. Remember, in Luke 9:1 He had given His disciples power to heal the sick, to cast out devils, and to preach the Gospel. Why could they not do that in this case? They lacked the two things they needed most, faith and prayer. These two things unlock the treasure chest in the heart of the Father. At this point in their lives, they lacked a consistent prayer life. Therefore, they lacked power. This was their kryptonite.

THEY LACKED THE TWO THINGS THEY NEEDED MOST, FAITH AND PRAYER. THESE TWO THINGS UNLOCK THE TREASURE CHEST IN THE HEART OF THE FATHER. AT THIS POINT IN THEIR LIVES, THEY LACKED A CONSISTENT PRAYER LIFE. THEREFORE, THEY LACKED POWER. THIS WAS THEIR KRYPTONITE.

Yet, because of the father's love for his son, he refused to give up, much like our Heavenly Father's love for us which never gives up, EVER. Although the boy's father was hurt and confused, he found the strength to run to Jesus. A large crowd gathered out of great curiosity to see if Jesus could do what no one up until this point had been able to do. The father was open, honest, and vulnerable when meeting Jesus. As children of God, we must do the same if we desire our prayers to be effective. We must remember: He sees us, knows us, and deeply understands and is acquainted with our sorrows. Our pains also trouble Him. We must know that He will never give up on us. The son was helpless and couldn't run to Christ, so the father had to run to Jesus for him. The question is, for whom will you run to Christ? Who is waiting for you to take the step of faith on their behalf? This is where we all long to be.

We want to be carriers of the presence of God for those who can't carry themselves. David said in Psalm 84:10, "For a day in Your courts is better than a thousand. I would rather be a doorkeeper in the house of my God than dwell in the tents of wickedness" (NKJV). He was simply saying, I want to be someone who holds the door open for those who are lost, struggling, and looking for a way home, a way into the presence of the Lord.

The father came face to face with the only person on the planet who could help him. This is where the father's desperation came alive. He saw the Creator of the heavens and the earth, the Author of life, the great King, and humanity's Savior; yet, even in this, he still had a seed of doubt. The father had heard the whispers and stories that this man, this Jesus, had healed the sick, opened blind eyes; He had made the deaf hear. It was rumored that He had fed 5,000 men, not counting women and children; it was also said that He had once defied the laws of gravity and walked on water to rescue His disciples. And yet, despite all this, the boy's father was still plagued with seeds of doubt, wondering, can He do a miracle for me?

This is where most of us find ourselves at some point, and maybe you, the reader, find yourself now. I know and truly believe He can do it for others, that He's performed miracles before, but is it possible that He would do one for me? Again, this is where faith, mixed with prayer, is your spiritual nuclear weapon.

As we see in verse 25, when God answers prayers, He doesn't answer them halfheartedly. He does a complete work. Jesus demanded that the demon come out of the child and never enter him again. That boy was forever changed because of one encounter with Christ. You, too, can be forever changed by one encounter with Christ. Your friend, family member, neighbor, coworker, the one God assigns you to carry into His presence, will be forever changed because of one encounter. The father's faith, bundled with prayer, changed his boy's life.

This type of encounter will not only change your family and friends but also you forever. As this story concludes, we see the disciples go to Jesus with the question that puzzled all twelve of them: Why could we not do this? Jesus' simple answer was their lack of prayer. "This kind can be cast out only by prayer" (Mark 9:29 NLT). If you're wondering why there might not be a specific breakthrough in an area of your life, maybe plant these words on the front porch of your heart. May I find myself at the feet of Christ, offering up my prayers like that father, "I believe; help my unbelief" (Mark 9:24 NKJV).

We must remember what the writer of Hebrews said: "But without faith it is impossible to please Him, for he who comes to God must believe that He is, and that He is a rewarder of those who diligently seek Him" (Hebrews 11:6 NKJV).

What's the reward? Him! He is the reward, presence, goodness, and grace in your life. He is the reward we are all looking for. We must come to Him by faith, continually pursuing Him daily. God framed the world with His words and invites us to frame our world with our prayers.

WHAT'S THE REWARD? HIM! HE IS THE REWARD, PRESENCE, GOODNESS, AND GRACE IN YOUR LIFE. HE IS THE REWARD WE ARE ALL LOOKING FOR. WE MUST COME TO HIM BY FAITH, CONTINUALLY PURSUING HIM DAILY. GOD FRAMED THE WORLD WITH HIS WORDS AND INVITES US TO FRAME OUR WORLD WITH OUR PRAYERS.

Just like Jesus said in Matthew 6:8, the Heavenly Father knows what you require before you ask, but according to James 4:3, you have not because you ask not. We must boldly, yet with humility, go to our Father in faith through the vehicle of prayer. He's waiting to speak with us.

He invites us to call out to Him, to pray to Him, and then He says if we will do this, the result will be that He will show us great and mighty things which we do not know! This is praying in faith, knowing God will move on our behalf.

Faith and prayer together are two potent powers for God's people to possess, and, if they resolve to believe, faith and prayer will be cultivated and will develop over time. Life's hardships, grief, illness, worry, pain, and heartache all contribute to the development of our faith and to our awareness of the necessity of prayer. God's Word provides a rich biblical catalog of amazing promises of how faith and prayer can change our lives.

Understanding Faith

What is faith, and how does it function with prayer? "Faith" is one of those words that is commonly used but not always precisely understood. Wayne Grudem's book on systematic theology frames the definition this way: "Trust or dependence on God based on the fact that we take him at his word and believe what he has said."

If you want to understand biblical faith, begin with Hebrews 11. This is known as the Faith Chapter, not because it features perfect men and women, but because God demonstrated His power through normal people having great faith. These ordinary men and women accomplished extraordinary feats with their lives simply because they all had one thing in common: They believed and had faith in God.

You don't have to live a perfect life, but you have to have perfect faith. Whether you're a prostitute, an 80-year-old stuttering shepherd, or whether you're jacked-up Samson, the common denominator in all these stories is faith.

The idea is, as long as I trust God, as long as I have faith, I know that I know that He will come through. He will respond to the faith that is embedded in my heart and seeps out through my prayers. As my spiritual father, Reinhard Bonnke, used to say, "If you want to deal with men, you need money, but if you want to deal with God, you need faith. For faith is God's address." Romans 10:17 says that faith comes by hearing and hearing by the Word of God.

THE LORD CONTINUOUSLY BIRTHS FAITH IN THE YIELDED BELIEVER SO THEY CAN KNOW WHAT HE PREFERS AND UNDERSTAND THE PERSUASION OF HIS WILL.

The Greek word "pistis" means faith, belief, trust, confidence, fidelity, and faithfulness, according to *Strong's Concordance*. Faith is always a gift from God and never something people can produce. In short, faith, for the believer, is "God's divine persuasion," distinct from human belief (confidence), yet involving it. The Lord continuously births faith in the yielded believer so they can know what He prefers and understand the persuasion of His will. "For whatever is born of God overcomes the world. And this is the victory that has overcome the world—our faith" (1 John 5:4 NKJV).

What does a life of faith look like? Let's go all the way back to Abraham, who was called the friend of God. When Abraham was 75 years old, God promised he would become a father to many nations (Genesis 12). Yet, we see in Genesis 18, six chapters later, that Abraham was now ninety-nine years of age, and this holy promise had seemed to evade him. He still didn't have a child, so he and Sarah's hearts had become flooded with doubt. At this stage in his life, he might have thought, "I'm okay; I obviously missed God. Maybe I didn't understand what He was saying. Sarah can't have kids; it's okay." He might have come to a place of peace where, even though he loved God, he recognized that maybe he had missed the boat.

How many of us have come to a place where we feel we have missed God? We weren't supposed to do this, go here, or take this job. Abraham had reconciled in his heart that maybe he had just missed the window of blessing. God had been faithful to him his whole life, but at this age, the promise he had received twenty-four years earlier had eluded him. BUT GOD. When he least expected it, God came and visited him, and Abraham rushed to host the presence of the Lord. In this moment of conversation, God spoke to Abraham and renewed the promise He had given years before. Meanwhile, as Sarah prepared a great meal for them, she heard the Lord deliver His promise again to Abraham and began to laugh, thinking, "I'm eighty-nine years old, and Abraham is ninety-nine." She was sure this was impossible. But, in Genesis 18:14, God asked Abraham, "Is there anything too hard for the Lord?" Of course, ten months later, the promised child was born. Isaac's name meant laughter. God caused the couple to laugh again because He was faithful. God is faithful. As He repeated this characteristic to Isaiah, He also speaks the same to you. "For My thoughts are not your thoughts, Nor are your ways My ways," says the Lord. "For as the heavens are higher than the earth, so are My ways higher than your ways, and My thoughts than your thoughts" (Isaiah 55:8-9 NKJV). Jeremiah also took a page from Abraham's playbook and said in 32:17, "Ah, Lord God! Behold, You have made the heavens and the earth by Your great power and outstretched arm. There is nothing too hard for You." In the same chapter in verse 27, God replied, "Behold, I am the Lord, the God of all flesh. Is there anything too hard for Me?" It's the same thing He told Abraham. Then, in the next chapter, 33:3, God invited Jeremiah into a beautiful and intimate conversation, saying, "Call to Me, and I will answer you, and show you great and mighty things, which you do not know" (NKJV).

The Lord is saying the same thing to you today. Come to Him in faith, knowing your prayers are received and answered, knowing there is nothing too hard for the Lord. Know today that God has invited you into His secret chambers, so approach His throne of grace with boldness. Come to Him through the corridors of Heaven, knowing that there's nothing that will be impossible for Him, that He will show you great and mighty things, that the moment your prayers leave your lips, God is coming with an answer. Daniel was well acquainted with this (Daniel 10:12). Know that the answer may not be in your timing, but it will come. This is where faith and prayer are married, in the secret place of Heaven. This is where God's heart comes alive when His children take Him at His word.

This is the crossroad where most believers find themselves: between the road of knowing and believing that God sees us, hears us, and is with us, and the other road where we are still in the valley of decision trying to reconcile our disappointment and understand why some of our prayers have gone unanswered. Is He still interested? Is He even concerned?

Just as the Lord invited the prophet Isaiah into a deep and intimate conversation with Him, He's inviting you and me to be with Him. "'Come now, and let us reason together,' says the Lord" (Isaiah 1:18 NKJV). God is continually inviting us to come away with Him, to be together as He told Isaiah. He wants you to come away from distractions, away from the noise and chaos of life, to simply rest with Him. Let Him pour His heart out to you. This can only be done in the secret place of prayer.

Spirit of Prayer and Faith

"Pray in the Spirit at all times in every prayer and supplication. To that end, keep alert and always persevere in supplication for all the saints" (Ephesians 6:18 NRSV). The total context of this verse is contained in Ephesians 6:10-20, in which God's people are instructed to put on the whole armor of God because of the cosmic powers of darkness. After putting on the armor of God, the last weapon of war is the Spirit of prayer.

Verses 16 and 17 are the connecting force. "With all of these, take the **shield of faith**, with which you will be able to quench all the flaming arrows of the evil one. Take the **helmet of salvation** and the **sword of the Spirit**, which is the word of God" (NRSV, emphasis added).

Prayer and the Word cannot be separated. The Gospel of John, verse 1:1, says, "In the beginning was the Word, and the Word was with God, and the Word was God," and in verse 14 it says, "And the Word became flesh and dwelt among us" (NKJV). This is a blueprint for prayer. When we pray, we should pray the Word. It's almost like we need to remind ourselves of the promises God has given us.

Some scholars believe there are over 7,000 promises in the Bible. To understand the promises God has laid out for us, we must carve out time to meditate on the Living Word. Therefore, when we pray, our prayers should reflect His promises, "God, you promised me joy, so why am I downcast? You promised to give me the desires of my heart, so why am I lonely?" Some of us have not seen the promises of God fulfilled in our lives because we lack quality time in the Word. God spoke to me years ago: "Bernie, when you lack spending time reading My Word, you're neglecting spending time with Me. I am the Word." If there are struggles in your life and problems that have gone unanswered, maybe the first place you should look is the Scriptures. Hebrews 4:12 says, "For the word of God is living and powerful, and sharper than any two-edged sword, piercing even to the division of soul and spirit, and of joints and marrow, and is a discerner of the thoughts and intents of the heart" (NKJV). The Word of God is the foundation of our faith. We must remember it's alive! It's the only book that, every time you open it, will speak to you. It's God-breathed. It's His heart on full display in sixty-six different books. It's His diary to you. Therefore, when you pray, your prayer should be aligned with His Word, for they go hand in hand.

We experience the Spirit through faith. The Greek "huperentugchano" means to make a petition or intercede on behalf of another. When you don't know how to pray, the Spirit will intervene for you. "Now, in the same way, the Spirit also helps our weakness; for we do not know what to pray for as we should, but the Spirit Himself intercedes for us with groanings too deep for words" (Romans 8:26 NASB).

The weakness mentioned here is defined by the prayers spoken when we need His power. The conditions here are not physical but spiritual. When we don't know where to turn, we have a Helper to build our faith and heal our pain. As the great apostle Paul encourages us: Never give up praying; pray always, and pray without ceasing (1 Thessalonians 5:17).

God wants us to ask, but sometimes the situation is too complex or troubles us to the point that we don't know what to pray for. We feel stuck. We have all experienced situations in which we wondered how to pray specifically. We don't know what would be best, nor do we understand the will of God for this specific issue or situation at hand. Yet we press on by faith and choose to pray. The apostle Paul says we do not know what to pray for as we ought. We lack wisdom. This is where faith comes in. Just like James says in Chapter 4, "You do not have, because you do not ask. You ask and do not receive, because you ask wrongly, to spend it on your passions" (James 4:2-3 ESV).

God wants us to pray, and we are constantly encouraged to pray. Jesus made it a priority to pray; He worded it, "when we pray," not, "if we pray," but, "when we pray." This was His constant theme. He lived a life of prayer. He prayed, then preached, healed, and delivered. Even when we do not have the words, having the faith and courage to come to God in prayer can move mountains. "So Jesus answered and said to them, 'Have faith in God. For assuredly, I say to you, whoever says to this mountain, "Be removed and be cast into the sea," and does not doubt in his heart but believes that those things he says will be done, he will have whatever he says. Therefore I say to you, whatever you ask when you pray, believe that you receive them, and you will have them'" (Mark 11:22-24 NKJV).

The Word of God in Psalm 119:130 instructs us that, "The unfolding of Your words gives light; It gives understanding to the simple" (NASB). You see, He is a constant help to us. The Spirit will guide you into all truth and will reveal things to you hidden from your natural mind and heart. "However, when He, the Spirit of truth, has come, He will guide you into all truth; for He will not speak on His own authority, but whatever He hears, He will speak; and He will tell you things to come. He will glorify Me, for He will take of what is Mine and declare it to you" (John 16:13, 14 NKJV). We can have faith that we do not pray into a void alone!

Faith is the fuel that propels even the smallest of prayers into the throne room of Heaven. Never doubt the power your prayers have when you ask in faith.

Faith is the fuel that propels even the smallest of prayers into the throne room of Heaven.

Chapter Three

The Secret Place

"He who dwells in the secret place of the Most High Shall abide under the shadow of the Almighty."
(Psalms 91:1 NKJV)

Imagine yourself driving down the road on a trip. In the natural, you see your gas gauge getting lower and lower. We all know a car has limited power to propel itself forward, so you pull over to a gas station and refuel to get to where you're headed. Much like a car, we aim for an eternal landing spot. Different seasons of life will lead us to different destinations. Still, ultimately, the journey will seem impossible unless we regularly carve out time to allow our spirit man to refuel. The secret place is our refueling station.

Jesus persistently displayed a prayer life in the secret place while He was on earth. He would escape to be alone with the Father, often in the wilderness or on a mountain and in the morning or at night, slipping away from the noise and distractions of everyday life to hide away in the wilderness and pray (Luke 5:16).

Often, we see that before the sun even rose, while it was still dark, Jesus got up, left the house, went away to a secluded place, and prayed (Mark 1:35). Other times, Jesus would ascend the mountain to speak to the Father. One time, in particular, He prayed all night for the disciples. After this prayer meeting, He made His final decision about them. Essentially, He prayed for one hour for each disciple. "It was at this time that He went off to the mountain to pray, and He spent the whole night in prayer to God" (Luke 6:12 NASB).

The traditional Jewish thought is that Moses wrote Psalm 91 about the secret place and penned these poetic words: "He who dwells in the secret place of the Most High Shall abide under the shadow of the Almighty" (Psalm 91:1 NKJV). The secret place is a picture of our time spent alone with God in prayer. In Psalm 91, Moses tells us that the depth of our walk with Jesus and the fruit of our lives depends on our time spent in the secret place.

In both the Old and New Testaments, Scripture often uses the term "secret place" to convey a solitary place away from any distractions. Some translations use the phrase "secret place" and translate it into "shelter," "covering," or "dwelling," but the meaning is the same. When you're with a loved one, there is a longing in your heart to just be with them. There is a passion deep within you that cries out for their attention. In much the same way, God has a deep passion to be with you!

WHEN YOU'RE WITH A LOVED ONE, THERE IS A LONGING IN YOUR HEART TO JUST BE WITH THEM. THERE IS A PASSION DEEP WITHIN YOU THAT CRIES OUT FOR THEIR ATTENTION. IN MUCH THE SAME WAY, GOD HAS A DEEP PASSION TO BE WITH YOU!

"For in the day of trouble He will conceal me in His tabernacle; In the secret place of His tent He will hide me; He will lift me up on a rock" (Psalms 27:5 NASB).

He will keep me secretly in His tabernacle—What David is saying is not that he would be physically hidden, but rather that his spirit would find great refuge in God in times of trouble. David knew all too well there was tremendous blessing and protection for the one who earnestly sought God. It wasn't a promise that God would prevent trouble from occurring, but rather that He would give security and blessing in the middle of it.

He will hide me in the secret place of His tent—There is a component of action and reaction in the secret place. As we continually pursue Him, the secret place of His presence opens to us, and we discover the glorious treasure awaiting us. The answers to the questions we have and the problems that trouble us dissipate as we linger in the secret place. We also take for granted the weight of glory in this tent. The Hebrew word here for "tent" or "dwelling place" also means "tabernacle," a holy place where the presence of God dwelt in the Old Testament. Here, we don't simply meet with a friend; we meet with the Alpha and Omega, the Creator, the Great King of Kings and Lord of Lords. We are elevated into His holy presence when we choose to meet with Him alone. In the Old Testament, the high priest could only walk into the Holy of Holies once a year to meet with God, but when Jesus came and died on that rugged cross, the veil was torn from top to bottom, giving us access, twenty-four hours a day, seven days a week, into the Holy of Holies, to meet with God Almighty. The question is, will you take advantage of your access?

Mountains and Hills—The Secret Place of God

In Scripture, mountains and hills were considered places close to God. Undoubtedly, the greatest mountain mentioned in the Bible is Mount Sinai. This is the same mountain where God first appeared to Moses in a flame of fire through a burning bush. Here, God spoke to him and laid out His rescue plan for the children of Israel. It's also the mountain where Moses took the children of Israel right after they journeyed through the Red Sea. Once they had arrived in the wilderness, Moses would experience the secret places on Mount Sinai more than any other prophet.

Moses' secret place wasn't necessarily a tent or a closet; his secret place was found on a mountain with the Creator. Years later, we discover the instructions that God divinely gave him through a meeting in the secret place, to build a tabernacle where God's presence could dwell. Moses shifted his secret place from the mountaintop to this holy tent, which became God's new dwelling place. Here, we see repeated encounters between God the Father and His servant Moses.

THE SECRET PLACE IS NOT A PARTICULAR LOCATION; THE SECRET PLACE IS WHEREVER GOD IS.

The secret place is not a particular location; the secret place is wherever God is. Sometimes we get caught up in thinking we need a special room or a prayer closet to meet with God. But, let me tell you, your car can become your tabernacle on your way to work; a walking trail or a park can bring you into communion with God. For Moses, it was a mountaintop. Where is it for you?

Mount Sinai—Moses' Secret Place

God met with Moses about eight times on this special mountain. As Moses ascended the mountain to meet with God, our Father also descended to meet with His son. The children of Israel were set free because of one man's obedience to God in the secret place. God demonstrated His power against the pharaoh, set His people free, and swung open the Red Sea. Everything began in a secret place. Three days after the Israelites wandered into the wilderness, Moses experienced the power of God on the mountain (Exodus 19:16). This set the precedent for how holy it is to hear from God. And yet, we take it for granted when we have free access to Him!

If a husband and wife don't talk often, it won't take long for them to be distressed when trouble strikes. Much like this example, if you don't commune with Christ before a time of trouble, you will not reap the benefits of His presence, His goodness, and His grace. Nurture and place great value on spending time with Him before you make a request for Him to answer any of your prayers. Make plans to meet with Him daily before you find yourself in a crisis.

God called Moses up the mountain several times, including the occasion on which He gave him the Ten Commandments, the spiritual and moral road map for life. Finally, in Exodus 33, God spoke over Moses in the secret place, tenderly and warmly. These were the last words God spoke to Moses before his death: "'But,' he said, 'You cannot see my face, for no man shall see Me and live.' And the Lord said, 'Behold, there is a place by me where you shall stand on the rock, and while my glory passes by, I will put you in a cleft of the rock, and I will cover you with my hand until I have passed by'" (Exodus 33:20-22 ESV). His graciousness allowed Moses to experience what no man had ever experienced since Adam in the Garden of Eden. It's in the secret place where we truly see the heart of God: He desires to meet with us in ways we cannot even fathom.

Jesus' Secret Place

Jesus spent much of His time in the secret place of prayer, and when He was not there, He taught others how to pray. In Mark 1, Jesus went to pray in a secret place, which was difficult for Him. "Now in the morning, having risen a long while before daylight, He went out and departed to a solitary place, and there He prayed. And Simon and those who were with Him searched for Him. When they found Him, they said to Him, 'Everyone is looking for You'" (Mark 1:35-36 NKJV).

Jesus didn't climb up to escape His peers; He wanted to draw near to His Father alone, just the two of them. But why not just lie there in His bed to pray? There is a reason to pray in a solitary secret place. "But now even more the report about him went abroad, and great crowds gathered to hear him and to be healed of their infirmities. But he would withdraw to desolate places and pray" (Luke 5:15-16 ESV). He often withdrew to lonely, secret places and prayed. Consider these words of praying in secret as mentioned in Matthew 6:6: "But when you pray, go into your room and shut the door and pray to your Father who is in secret. And your Father who sees in secret will reward you" (ESV).

Notice the descriptions Jesus used to emphasize how being alone with your Father is its own reward. "Go into your room" and "close the door" to "pray to your Father who is in secret" but who "sees" in that secret place. To Jesus, prayer is when the infinite God is alone with me — looking at me intently and intimately as if it's just Him and me, all alone "in secret."

After Jesus performed the miracle of feeding over 5,000 people, He dismissed the crowd so that He could pray. He went up to the mountain alone, and when the evening came, He was there by Himself (Matthew 14:22-23).

Mount of Olives—Place of Prayer

One of the most famous landmarks in the Bible is the Mount of Olives, serving as a divide between the sacred Temple Mount and the Judean desert. This area holds profound religious significance as the site where Jesus ascended into Heaven, according to Acts 1:11, and it is anticipated to be the place of His future return.

Initially used as a sanctuary for prayer, the Mount of Olives saw King David's barefoot ascent in prayer as he sought to hide from his son Absalom's wrath (1 Samuel 15:30). This sacred hill also served as the backdrop for the prophetic statements of Zechariah and Ezekiel, which predicted judgment upon Israel and the eventual restoration and regathering of the exiled people. Notably, Zechariah pinpointed the Mount of Olives as the precise location of the Messiah's return (Zechariah 14:4).

The route to Jerusalem rises steadily from the Dead Sea, twelve miles away at 1,200 feet below sea level, to the Mount of Olives, rising 200 feet above the Old City to an elevation of 2,700 feet. Jesus turned His attention to making this final climb.

When Jesus arrived in Jerusalem on the week of the Passover, He chose the Mount of Olives as His staging ground for His time in the city. From this mountain, Jesus rode a donkey into the town, cheered on by shouts of hallelujah and waving palm branches, and from this mountain, Jesus looked out over Jerusalem and wept over this world that He dearly loved. From the garden at the base of this mountain, Jesus prayed in secret to God on the night of His arrest. After His death and resurrection, Jesus invited His disciples to join Him one last time, again on the Mount of Olives.

The Secret of the Ancient Ways

"Stand by the ways and see and ask for the ancient paths, Where the good way is, and walk in it; Then you will find a resting place for your souls" (Jeremiah 6:16 NASB).

Much time had passed, but Peter remembered the ancient paths of climbing the mountain to Mount Sinai, the secret place where he had found a resting place for his soul, free from the memories he had in the past on God's mountain. The sacred events on the Mount of Transfiguration solidified Simon Peter's authority to lead the embryonic church.

Through remembering the scriptural account of the transfiguration, with Old Testament parallels and modern revelation, Peter received the authority and the governing keys requisite to lead the kingdom of God on earth.

In his second epistle, Peter referred to his experience on the Mount of Transfiguration as an event at which he obtained not only a more sure word of prophecy but also the authority to interpret Scripture. Peter opened the discussion of the transfiguration by encouraging the people to work to ensure their salvation so that they might receive an inheritance in the kingdom of God. "Therefore, brethren, be all the more diligent to make certain about His calling and choosing you; for as long as you practice these things, you will never stumble; for in this way the entrance into the eternal kingdom of our Lord and Savior Jesus Christ will be abundantly supplied to you" (2 Peter

1:10-11 NASB). He taught that he wished the people to retain in their memories his witness of the glory of Jesus and that he expected his death shortly.

Intimacy with God—Secret Place of the Stairs

"O my dove, that art in the clefts of the rock, in the secret places of the stairs, let me see thy countenance, let me hear thy voice; for sweet is thy voice, and thy countenance is comely" (Song of Solomon 2:14).

The great Lover of our souls sees us as a dove hidden in the clefts of the rock. As God said to Moses, "I will put you in a cleft of the rock, and will cover you with My hand" (Exodus 33:22 NKJV).

Who is that Rock? "…and all drank the same spiritual drink. For they drank of that spiritual Rock that followed them, and that Rock was Christ" (1 Corinthians 10:4 NKJV).

Christ was perfected in His love for us by His suffering to bring us to Himself and was the Rock crushed to provide living water for us. The sword that pierced His side opened a cleft where the waters gushed out and where we may hide. Jesus sees us as His glorious dove, hidden at His side!

"Surely he has borne our griefs And carried our sorrows; Yet we esteemed him stricken, Smitten by God, and afflicted. But he was wounded for our transgressions, He was bruised for our iniquities; The chastisement for our peace was upon him, and by His stripes, we are healed" (Isaiah 53:4-5 NKJV).

> "To fall in love with God is the greatest of all romances; to seek Him, the greatest adventure; to find Him, the greatest human achievement."

One of the ancient church fathers, St. Augustine of Hippo, wrote these words to express his love for God: "To fall in love with God is the greatest of all romances; to seek Him, the greatest adventure; to find Him, the greatest human achievement."

You might not know it, but Jesus is knocking at the door of our hearts, and I wonder if we are opening the door to receive Him for moments of intimacy with Him. Jack Deere wrote these words on deep love for Jesus:

"I want passionate feelings to characterize my relationship with the Lord Jesus. Of course, I want to be perfectly obedient to the Lord, but I want the obedience to spring out of passionate love for Him. I want to obey Jesus not simply out of discipline of duty or because of some reward or fear of punishment. I want to serve Him simply for the joy of being able to please the one I love so much. If discipline is what ultimately drives us in our pursuit of Jesus, eventually we will give up that pursuit. But a man in love, or a woman in love, will never quit—I want my life to be characterized by an unrestrained affection for the Son of God."

The secret places of the stairs—When Jacob was fleeing from Esau, he was so drained that the first night he used rocks for pillows, and they couldn't keep him awake! He dreamed about a ladder reaching up to heaven with angels ascending and descending on it. The Lord stood above and said to him, "I am with you and will watch over you wherever you go, and I will bring you back to this land. I will not leave you until I have done what I have promised you" (Genesis 28:15 NIV). This evokes Solomon's promise to his wife and the promise Jesus made to us: "Go therefore and make disciples of all the nations, baptizing them in the name of the Father and of the Son and of the Holy Spirit, teaching them to observe all things that I have commanded you; and lo, **I am with you always**, even to the end of the age" (Matthew 28:19-20 NKJV, emphasis added).

God is love—that's His heart, His very nature. As a flower unfolds in response to the warm sun and rain showers, we respond to God's love in the secret place. "Beloved, let us love one another, for love is from God, and whoever loves has been born of God and knows God.

GOD IS LOVE—THAT'S HIS HEART, HIS VERY NATURE. AS A FLOWER UNFOLDS IN RESPONSE TO THE WARM SUN AND RAIN SHOWERS, WE RESPOND TO GOD'S LOVE IN THE SECRET PLACE.

Anyone who does not love does not know God because God is love. In this, the love of God was made manifest among us, that God sent his only Son into the world so that we might live through him" (1 John 4:7-9 ESV).

We love best when love fills our hearts. An empty cup cannot quench thirst; only one full of water or another kind of liquid can. To be full of love is to spend time contemplating and experiencing the God of love. How do we reach this point? We do it through prayer and meditation on the Word of God. "The Lord would speak to Moses face to face, as one speaks to a friend" (Exodus 33:11 NIV).

As the Lord demonstrated His love to Moses, so should we show our love for God. When you live in the secret place of prayer in the presence of God, your heart will open up so you can express your love for Him.

In my own secret place, I write down prayers and wait for the Lord to answer me. In Habakkuk, the prophet inquired of the Lord and wrote the Lord's response on his tablet. Jesus said His sheep know His voice.

God's voice to us calms and edifies. It encourages and woos us. All is well when you are in the secret place.

Chapter Four

Conversations with God

"Don't ever hesitate to take to [God] whatever is on your heart. He already knows it anyway, but He doesn't want you to bear its pain or celebrate its joy alone."
- Billy Graham

What would God's voice sound like when He has a conversation? Some seem to discern God's voice as sounding like a wave when it hits the shore of our minds. It is certain that the voice of God ebbs and flows in our conversations. One of the benefits of conversation with God is that He constantly speaks to us and gives us His direction. It's never the Lord who is not speaking; it is we who are not hearing.

Jesus made some radical statements about hearing His voice. Jesus uses John 10:3-5 as a metaphor to make a statement about knowing His voice. "The gatekeeper opens the gate for him, and the sheep listen to his voice. He calls his own sheep by name and leads them out. When he has brought out all his own, he goes on ahead of them, and his sheep follow him because they know his voice. But they will never follow a stranger; in fact, they will run away from him because they do not recognize a stranger's voice" (NIV). Proximity produces closeness. In other words, the closer you are to Him, the easier it is to hear His voice. One of the greatest prophets we read about in the Old Testament is Samuel. Samuel's mother was named Hannah. You likely remember the story of Hannah crying out to the Lord for a child. This happened repeatedly, and despite the constant silence she felt in response to the prayers she prayed, she refused to give up. She knew the Lord would one day answer the deep cries of her heart! And boy, did He ever answer her! He gave her a son, and she gave him back to the Lord as an offering after she had weaned him. He grew up in the house of God, learning to pray and listen to the voice of our Heavenly Father. Fast forward several years, and Samuel had unprecedented influence over the nation of Israel. He was the one everyone went to in order to hear what the Lord was saying or to get direction for their lives. One day, the people came together and demanded that Samuel give them a king like all the other nations around them. They thought a king would help keep them safe from all of their enemies and bring stability and order to their everyday lives. Samuel rebuked them and tried to convince them that they were different from all the other nations. They were called and set apart by God; they were His treasure, His special people, His prized possession, and, ultimately, He—God Himself—was their king! He would always protect them. But, for whatever reason, that wasn't good enough for them. So, the Lord instructed Samuel where to find an earthly king for the Israelites. Scripture says in 1 Samuel 9:15 (NKJV) that the Lord "told Samuel in his ear." Samuel walked so close to God that God only needed to whisper, and Samuel would hear Him. I want to encourage you to walk so close to the Lord that He only needs to whisper for you to hear Him.

The Voice of God

Samuel heard a voice calling out to him, but he didn't recognize that it was the Lord who was doing the calling because he did not know the voice of God. Eli taught him the Word, and that's when things changed (1 Samuel 3:1-10). In the Bible, Samuel and Gideon both had issues with recognizing God. Gideon saw God in the flesh and still doubted what he had heard and asked for a sign, not once, but three times (Judges 6:17-22, 36-40). He experienced uncertainty about God several times: "And the Lord said to him, 'Surely I will be with you, and you shall defeat the Midianites as one man.' Then he said to Him, 'If now I have found favor in Your sight, then show me a sign that it is You who talk with me'" (Judges 6:16-17 NKJV).

When listening to God's voice, how can we know He is the one speaking? First of all, we have something that Gideon and Samuel did not. We have the complete Bible, the inspired Word of God, to read, study, and meditate on. "All Scripture is God-breathed and is useful for teaching, rebuking, correcting and training in righteousness, so that the servant of God may be thoroughly equipped for every good work" (2 Timothy 3:16-17 NIV). When people question God, the Bible reveals much of His character. Titus 1:2 gives us an answer to our wondering: "This truth gives them confidence that they have eternal life, which God—who does not lie—promised them before the world began" (NLT).

The Sound of the Lord

How is sound measured? To measure the intensity or noise level of a sound, we use a measurement unit called a decibel. Quite simply, the louder the sound, the higher the decibel number. The decibels of God range from the decibel of 30, which is a whisper, to the decibel of 120, which is thunder.

Zechariah 4:6 (NIV) tells us that God's work is "Not by might nor by power, but by My Spirit," meaning God does not always need to perform in supernatural, miraculous ways to get our attention, and He's certainly not relegated to always doing or speaking in the same manner as He's done in times past. He simply spoke at the beginning of time, and the creation process began. When He speaks, things happen. Isaiah tells us in chapter 55:11 that His Word will NEVER return void, that it will certainly accomplish what it was sent to accomplish.

You can rest assured that whatever promises God has given you, He will ensure they come to pass. No matter what! There's no room for DOUBT!

Interestingly, earlier in the chapter, the Lord invites us to come to Him, and He will speak to us, in verses 2-6:

> "Listen carefully to Me, and eat what is good, And let your soul delight itself in abundance. Incline your ear, and come to Me. Hear, and your soul shall live; And I will make an everlasting covenant with you—The sure mercies of David...Seek the Lord while He may be found, Call upon Him while He is near" (NKJV).

YOU MUST UNDERSTAND THAT THE LORD IS NOT PLAYING A GAME OF HIDE AND SEEK. HE PROMISES THAT IF YOU SEEK HIM, HE'LL FIND YOU, AND HE WILL SPEAK TO YOU. WHAT A GREAT PROMISE.

You must understand that the Lord is not playing a game of hide and seek. He promises that if you seek Him, He'll find you, and He will speak to you. What a great promise.

The God Who Speaks

It's safe to say all people would love to hear the audible voice of God. Saint Augustine was in his early forties when he wrote *Confessions*, a rich meditation by a middle-aged man on the meaning of his life. The contrast between his past journey and his later position of authority as bishop began when he unveiled his disappointment in waiting so long to hear God's voice. He wrote that one day, while sitting in his garden, he heard a child playing, motivating him to pick up his Bible and read. The words jumped off the pages, almost like he was being read a story. This changed his perspective on the voice of God. "You called and cried out loud and shattered my deafness. You were radiant and resplendent, you put to flight my blindness. You were fragrant, and I drew in my breath and now pant after you. I tasted you, and I feel but hunger and thirst for you. You touched me, and I am set on fire to attain the peace which is yours."

Charles Stanley asked a question in his book, *Prayer: The Ultimate Conversation*: "With whom are you speaking?" Why does he call this the ultimate conversation? Because of the Audience. If you sat down with me and told me you just met with the King of England for coffee, I would be extremely perplexed, and then I'd ask what he said! You would catch me in awe. What happened? How did you get his attention? It's the same thing with prayer. You can sit with the great King of the Universe, and so few of us take advantage of it because of our natural minds; God sent His Son to build His bridge from Heaven to Earth. You have the greatest Audience at hand.

Without God's voice, we would be unaware of His expectations for us and His provisions. Notice the power of God's Word: in the beginning, there was nothing—next to nothingness—until God identified His purposes. With just two words spoken by God, the light came into existence. God creates by speaking, making the world a reality through His spoken word.

Once God had created man and woman living in the garden of Eden, a world of people emerged, creating the opportunity to converse with God. David did amazing things for God and His people, but one thing that stands out in David's life more than anything else is his relationship with God, for the Scripture says he was a man after God's own heart. Being the psalmist he was, David often prayed by first entering God's presence with praise and thanksgiving. After that, he would make his requests known to the Lord as anyone else would, but often, in times of urgency, his requests would become a crying out to God rather than just a graceful plea.

There were moments when David would worship before the Lord to celebrate God's awesome words and actions—"Enter into His gates with thanksgiving, And into His courts with praise. Be thankful to Him, and bless His name" (Psalms 100:4 NKJV).

At other times, when anxious, David would call upon God— "In my distress I called upon the Lord, And cried out to my God; He heard my voice from His temple, And my cry came before Him, even to His ears" (Psalms 18:6 NKJV).

God cares enough about us to reveal Himself to us. Still, we cannot have a relationship with God without grasping His words. God doesn't always profoundly speak to us as He did with Moses, speaking from a burning bush. Not all of us will experience something like Moses' or Paul's dynamic experience when he was close to Damascus. Paul experienced a dramatic conversation with Jesus. "...suddenly, a light from heaven flashed around him. And falling to the ground, he heard a voice saying to him, 'Saul, Saul, why are you persecuting me?'" Paul wasn't certain who this person was, maybe an angel. "And he said, 'I am Jesus, whom you are persecuting. But rise and enter the city, and you will be told what you are to do'" (Acts 9:3-6 ESV). Jesus spoke these words in the conversation, and Paul only said three words. The spoken words of Jesus would alter Paul's life, and then he would change the world for Jesus, all made possible by that short conversation.

The God Who Answers

If you walk daily with the Lord and demonstrate obedience to Him, you will see His supernatural intervention. In the Old Testament, God responded to Nehemiah's faith. He was a man set on rebuilding the fallen wall of Jerusalem. For quite some time, Nehemiah prayed to the Lord and, at great risk to himself, asked Him to grant favor with his boss, the earthly king, so that Nehemiah could go back and rebuild Jerusalem's walls. Because of his continued pursuit of God in prayer, he was granted supernatural favor.

When things are bothering you, you must know they are bothering God. You are His child, and He sees your heart. For instance, Nehemiah heard that the walls of the city he loved so much in his hometown were destroyed, and his distress also distressed God. God is not Santa Claus; it's not a one-and-done wish granted. Just like in the case of Nehemiah, there is a process of time. Nehemiah waited four months. For you, it could be four days, four weeks, or even four years, but you can rest assured that God will answer. Remember the persistent widow Jesus spoke about in Luke 18. The evil judge refused to help the poor woman, but she continued to ask for justice. "For some time he refused. But finally he said to himself, 'Even though I don't fear God or care what people think, yet because this widow keeps bothering me, I will see that she gets justice, so that she won't eventually come and attack me!'" (Luke 18:4-5 NIV). Jesus reminds us to keep asking, to keep knocking, for the door will certainly be opened.

In the same way, whether it's an issue at work, a project at school, a relationship with a friend, or a family issue, whatever issue is bothering you, it is bothering God. If your heart hurts, His heart is hurting, too. He is inviting you to come and ask Him for a resolution. Paul says to make your requests known to God. If you continually seek Him and go after Him, He will reward you. He will grant you your heart's desires.

IF YOUR HEART HURTS, HIS HEART IS HURTING, TOO. HE IS INVITING YOU TO COME AND ASK HIM FOR A RESOLUTION.

The God who answers— Daniel's great concern for his people was evident as he described a vision given to him by the Lord. At the time of this vision, Daniel was approximately 85 years old.

It had been about a year since almost 50,000 Jews had returned to rebuild their country and the temple. Daniel had probably heard the people faced obstacles in rebuilding the temple, and he knew the tough challenges that awaited them. He believed in God, but he must have wondered how everything would work out in light of the prophecy of Jeremiah. The answer to your heart's desire is often found through the journey of waiting.

"In the first year of his reign I, Daniel, understood by the books the number of the years specified by the word of the Lord through Jeremiah the prophet, that He would accomplish seventy years in the desolations of Jerusalem" (Daniel 9:2 NKJV). Would those people who returned to Israel trust God?

At this time, Daniel had such questions that the Lord answered and gave a vision to the prophet. He was certain "the thing was true, but the time appointed was long" (Daniel 10:1 KJV). He understood that he would not be able to see all of God's plans unfold, but Daniel believed everything would happen according to the will of God. Here is an illustration of our prayer life. We get caught up in the enemy's lies that if our prayers are not answered immediately, we must not be praying for God's will. We have forgotten the art of Jacob, of wrestling with God. Jacob sent his wife, kids, and servants away, and the Scripture says he was alone with God. There, in that place, he wrestled with God. God told him, "Let me go, for the day breaks." Jacob said, "I will not let you go unless you bless me!" (Genesis 32:26 NKJV). There's nothing new under the sun; this was the first UFC match. God broke Jacob's hip. But, it was through this wrestling match that he was named Israel. This is significant because Jacob's name meant "deceiver." But, after this fight, he was renamed Israel, meaning "one with God." The beauty of waiting is knowing that one wrestling match with God will change who you are. One night with the King, your past will be forgotten, and your future will be rewritten.

> THE BEAUTY OF WAITING IS KNOWING THAT ONE WRESTLING MATCH WITH GOD WILL CHANGE WHO YOU ARE. ONE NIGHT WITH THE KING, YOUR PAST WILL BE FORGOTTEN, AND YOUR FUTURE WILL BE REWRITTEN.

The unexpected answers of God—In John 16:23-24 (ESV), Jesus made a stunning promise, which applies to all of us who believe in Him: "In that day, you will ask nothing of me. Truly, truly, I say to you, whatever you ask of the Father in my name, he will give it to you. Until now, you have asked nothing in my name. Ask, and you will receive that your joy may be full." The problem doesn't lie with Jesus ignoring our prayers; the problem lies with us not asking. Here, He is inviting us to ask! "Whatever" means whatever is on your heart, whatever is troubling your soul. What is it that's bothering you? Jesus is inviting us to make our petitions to God. Just as an earthly father doesn't want his child to bottle up all that is troubling him, we have a Heavenly Father who truly desires for you to pour out your heart and ask Him for whatever it is that you need. Jesus repeatedly says, "Until now, you've asked nothing!" Then, He makes a promise: Ask and you WILL receive; not, ask, and I'll think about it; not, ask, and I'll see what I can do or answer at some point. No, He says, ask, and you will receive, and when you receive the answers to your prayers, it's then that your joy will be full. He desires to see His children filled with happiness, but remember, God can't do much with what you don't give Him. Don't limit yourself from experiencing His fullness because you are holding back from asking your Father. So, ask!

God Speaks in Silence

Years ago, I went through a time when I felt like the Lord was silent. He just wasn't speaking to me like usual, and I didn't know why. I'd been faithfully praying, reading the Scriptures, worshipping, seeking, and searching, yet there was silence. "Lord, where are You?" Several days turned into weeks until finally, out of frustration, I cried, "Lord, speak to me—please! Where did You go?" The Lord whispered softly to me and said, "Bernie, sometimes I speak loudest in times of silence! I was with you all along." I was reminded of when Jesus got in the boat and told His disciples to follow Him, that they were going to the other side (Mark 4:35-41). The Scriptures say that it was evening time. Jesus was tired from many days of nonstop ministry, so He went to the back of the boat, grabbed a pillow, and fell asleep. As the disciples attempted to cross the Sea of Galilee, a storm arose out of nowhere. Storms were nothing new to the disciples. Most were fishermen, and these guys had been acquainted with the storms that arose on the sea of Galilee. But, on this particular night, the storm was much different than usual. This storm had a ferociousness these guys had never seen or dealt with before. They were overcome with fear, even fearing for their lives! Amid the waves crashing against their boats, they did what they thought they were supposed to do in the natural; they threw things overboard to lighten the load to make the boat more buoyant and thus easier to navigate through this horrific storm. However, their attempts failed. Nothing they did seemed to work. They soon realized, "This is it; we're doomed! We're not going to make it." I wonder if, for a split second, they thought to themselves, "How did this happen? He's the One who told us to get in the boat. We were just following His lead. He was the first one in the boat, and look where this has gotten us. We're going to die! Why is He not helping us? How can He be sleeping while we are dying? Doesn't He see what we're going through? I don't understand all this. All we did was follow His plans, leading us down this very troubling path." Yet, Jesus was on the boat all along.

Have you ever felt this way? Everything is going so well one day, and you are caught in a hurricane the next. The storms of life have become so ferocious that you're convinced you're doomed. You've tried everything you know to try, yet nothing is working. The waves of life are crashing all around you, and no matter what you do to fix things and stay afloat, you begin to drown in life's sorrows. "Lord, where are You? Why are You silent?" It's here that we must take a page out of the disciples' playbook and realize that not only does He care, but He's been in our boat all along. He's just a few inches away from us. You may think you're waiting on the Lord to move on your behalf, but it's actually the Lord waiting on you to get desperate enough to do what the disciples did. They ran to Jesus with utter desperation in their voices, like a bunch of middle school girls at a Justin Bieber concert. They went to Him, woke Him up, and screamed, "Don't You care that we are perishing?" Wiping the drool off His lips and chin, He got up and rebuked the wind and waves. The Bible says, "Immediately there was a great calm on the sea." The disciples looked at one another with absolute amazement and thought, "Who is this - that even the winds and the waves obey Him?"

They'd been wrestling for hours with this storm without ever thinking about waking Jesus up to deal with it. Maybe they, like many of us, thought, "He's been so busy lately; we'll just let Him sleep. He's really not interested in this kind of thing. He's got more important issues to deal with." In contrast, the Lord spoke to me many years ago and said, "Bernie, if it troubles you, then it troubles Me." You must know that the Lord is gentle, but He's also a giant. He's kind but ferocious, and, most of the time, He doesn't move on our behalf unless invited. You're not waiting on Him; He's waiting on you to invite Him into your situation.

> You must know that the Lord is gentle, but He's also a giant. He's kind but ferocious, and, most of the time, He doesn't move on our behalf unless invited. You're not waiting on Him; He's waiting on you to invite Him into your situation.

During the silence, the Lord was there all along. Yes, He speaks in the silence.

Friend of God

Have you ever really thought about, contemplated, or meditated on the depth of love Jesus has for you? I'm sure, at some point, that thought has crossed your mind, but I invite you to camp out for a minute at the thought of His deep love for you. Jesus Himself declares to a group of people in John 15:13, "Greater love has no one than this: to lay down one's life for one's friends" (NIV).

Jesus calls and identifies those who've been following Him as His friends. What an honor this must have been for His disciples. In His day, it was considered a great honor for a Jewish rabbi to call you friend, but for Jesus, who was not only a rabbi but also the one and only Son of God, to call those who faithfully followed Him His friends was an unfathomable honor. Jesus is calling us His friends, too. His love for us, His friends, is so grand that He's saying He will lay down His life for us! His followers could not possibly have fathomed the depth of that divine love. The great apostle Paul tried his best to put it into perspective when he told the Roman church this: "For scarcely for a righteous man will one die; yet perhaps for a good man someone would even dare to die. But God demonstrates His own love toward us, in that while we were still sinners, Christ died for us" (Romans 5:8 NKJV). You can sense in Paul's writing that he's trying his best to communicate God's great love to the reader, but it's as if he's still missing something. As brilliant a thinker and theologian as Paul was, he still fell short in describing Jesus' great love for us. So, once again, he attempted to tackle this theme of God's "great love" for you. Three chapters later in Romans chapter 8, he said, "And I am convinced that nothing can ever separate us from God's love. Neither death nor life, neither angels nor demons, neither our fears for today nor our worries about tomorrow—not even the powers of hell can separate us from God's love. No power in the sky above or in the earth below—indeed, nothing in all creation will ever be able to separate us from the love of God that is revealed in Christ Jesus our Lord" (Romans 8:38-39 NLT). You must do your best to understand that the love Jesus has for you is far greater than you could fathom. His love is simply incomprehensible, and He is beckoning you to realize that He views you in this relational light; He views you as His friend. Divinity befriending humanity, the Creator befriending creation. Nothing will ever be able to separate you from His indescribable love!

Everlasting Love

Jeremiah 31:3 tells us, "Long ago the Lord said to Israel: 'I have loved you, my people, with an everlasting love. With unfailing love I have drawn you to myself'" (NLT).

The greatest scientists of all time, using the most sophisticated instruments we have, can't come close to measuring the distance of "forever" between two objects. The distance between two opposing directions is simply immeasurable. Yet, the Lord tells David that He's removed our sins as far as the east is from the west (Psalms 103:12). What an immense promise the Lord has not only given David but also given to all of us. He reassures Micah that our sins have been cast into the sea of forgetfulness (Micah 7:19). What tremendous love

He displays. The Father will never bring up your sins, mistakes, or past failures. Instead, He'll continue to remind you of His everlasting love. That leads to the question, if the Lord doesn't bring up our past sins, why would we? Don't allow the guilt and shame of your past to hinder you from receiving His forgiveness and basking in the eternal glow of His everlasting love.

The enemy's only goal is for us to bask in the shame of our mistakes. From the very beginning of time, when Adam grasped for that first breath of air, when his heart pounded its first beat, God's number one goal was for His creation to know Him intimately, to know His glorious love deeply. Yet, when Adam and Eve fell, they ran and hid; they were ashamed and did their best to hide from God. He was the only One who could bring forgiveness, healing, and love. Although they covered themselves with shame, He covered them with grace and love. God's initial rebuke of their disobedience can read as though He had distanced Himself from them. However, we know the whole story! The Bible says God works all things together for the good of those called according to His purposes. Behind the discipline of Adam and Eve, God already had a plan meant for their redemption—not just theirs, but the whole world's! Don't ever think that God has stopped loving you. The eternal God has eternal plans that extend far beyond our understanding, and His plans are not void of His love. "For his anger lasts only a moment, but his favor lasts a lifetime; weeping may last for the night, but joy comes in the morning" (Psalms 30:5 NIV).

Just know He's longing to do the very same for you today. He desires to cover your shame, your guilt, and your sin with the precious blood of His Son. Therefore, if you find yourself in a similar place to Adam and Eve, don't run away from the Father; rather, run to Him. Run right into His everlasting arms of grace and love and receive the most incredible gift He so freely gives, forgiveness for your sin. Let Him remove that coat of guilt and shame and replace it with a glorious crown of grace and love.

Communicating with the Creator

Years ago, a friend of mine who worked at the same ministry I did sat down with me and said, "Bernie, you know how we always cry out to God and say, 'God! Answer the cries of my heart!'" I said, "Of course." He then said, "I felt God say to me, 'You always ask for Me to answer the cries of your heart; why don't you first answer the cries of My heart?'" So often, we forget Someone is listening at the other end of our prayers! And, much more than just a Someone, it's God, the One who Was, Is, and Always Will Be! He can and will intervene for us and instantly change our world. For this to happen, however, we must enter into conversation with Him.

We can't brush over the topic of speaking with the Lord without mentioning what God wants to share with His children. Often, we approach God with such a long laundry list of needs that we forget that there may be something He wants to tell us. Part of the art of conversation is listening. Prayer is not just telling God our needs but also listening to His desires for our lives. Allow God to reveal Himself to you. When you pray, ask God to share His heart with you! You may be surprised by how He responds.

Chapter Five

The Surrendered Life of Prayer

Though there are no words for surrender in the Bible, the Greek word "paradidomi" means to surrender, yield up, entrust, bring forth, deliver, give up, and put in prison. The word "surrendered" is mentioned in the book of Acts in one translation: "Men who have surrendered themselves for the name of our Lord Yeshua The Messiah" (Acts 15:26 Aramaic Bible in Plain English).

These men surrendered their lives, all for the name of Jesus, a noble testimony! Throughout the Bible, we read of ordinary men and women who decided to fully surrender their lives to the Lord—not once, but daily. The example these men and women provide is extraordinary.

You have probably heard about the "surrendered life," but I suspect most people know about it and don't know the richness of its meaning. As indicated in the above-mentioned translation, the surrendered life is giving back to Jesus the life He granted you. It involves relinquishing control, rights, power, direction, and everything you do and say, resigning your life to His hands as an instrument to change the world for Him. You may not realize that even Jesus lived the surrendered life, giving Himself for His Father's purposes. He does not call us to do anything that He has not done.

> **You may not realize that even Jesus lived the surrendered life, giving Himself for His Father's purposes. He does not call us to do anything that He has not done.**

The book of John powerfully describes Jesus, beginning with the reality that He surrendered His life in Heaven. "For I have come down from heaven, not to do my own will, but the will of him who sent me" (John 6:38 ESV).

Jesus also told the scribes and Pharisees that He had surrendered His life to His Father. "When you have lifted up the Son of Man, then you will know that I am he and that I do nothing on my own authority but speak just as the Father taught me. And he who sent me is with me. He has not left me alone, for I always do the things that are pleasing to him" (John 8:28-29 ESV).

Again, Jesus was living a life of surrender by honoring His Father, but others did not honor Jesus. So, Jesus said, "Yet I do not seek my glory; there is One who seeks it, and he is the judge" (John 8:50 ESV).

Sometimes, a life of surrender does not happen by choice, as it was with Peter: "So when he had arrested him, he put him in prison, and delivered (paradidomi) him to four squads of soldiers to keep him, intending to bring him before the people after Passover." But, as God worked Satan's intentions for good, what landed Peter in jail led the church to action. "Peter was therefore kept in prison, but constant prayer was offered to God for him by the church" (Acts 12:4-5).

The Surrendered Life—The Life of Prayer

How do we surrender our lives to God and live a life of prayer? These two concepts go together, but we must commit completely to surrender and to prayer.

> **A genuine decision to follow and obey God is a decision of total surrender. Many of us struggle to surrender all to God's will truly, but surrender is what sets us free.**

First, the radical act of surrender involves submitting your life to God. A genuine decision to follow and obey God is a decision of total surrender. Many of us struggle to surrender all to God's will truly, but surrender is what sets us free.

At the end of Genesis 11, we find Abram on the road to Canaan. He had just lost his brother and father when the Lord told him to go out away from his country "To a land that I will show you" (Genesis 12:1 NKJV). Abram is obedient despite leaving the only home he had ever known to follow God's promise of land for his descendants. There, Abram built an altar and worshipped the Lord (12:7). We know the whole story, that Abram gained not only a new name but the full promise that God had given him. Surrendering to God aligns your desires with God's desires and creates a willingness to follow Him as He guides you in your life.

In the most simplistic, elementary way, surrendering means simply giving up your will or desires for His! It's the mindset or act of allowing Him to lead you or guide you, daily, in everything you do. As believers, we simply surrender our will for His. No questions asked. We have the greatest power source at our disposal and know that we never have to journey this life alone.

"For I am the Lord your God who takes hold of your right hand and says to you, Do not fear; I will help you" (Isaiah 41:13 NIV).

"Trust in the Lord with all your heart, and do not lean on your own understanding. In all your ways acknowledge him, and he will make straight your paths" (Proverbs 3:5-6 ESV).

Here is the path of a surrendered life—listen to God and hear His words! The Lord will fight for you while you remain still, and when your eyes are looking in many directions and you are unsure, keep your eyes on the Lord, and you will not be surprised. When you sense your feet are slipping, the Lord's unfailing love is always there to hold you up.

Prayer is the second part of the surrendered life. We can have plans in the core of our hearts, but sometimes we lack the power to pray for what is truly best for us. Jesus scolded the disciples in the garden just before His death due to their inability to stay awake with Him and pray. "'The spirit indeed is willing but the flesh is weak,' Jesus said to them" (Matthew 26:41 NKJV). I still hear His thoughts echoing through many hearts today; He is bidding us to come away with Him to pray, talk, and communicate. Our prayers should reflect close alignment with His will for our lives, which can be difficult if we lack the discipline simply to speak with Him! The disciples knew just how vital this practice was, so they only asked Jesus to teach them to pray.

No matter how well prepared we are or how much we plan and organize, life is full of unexpected change, uncertainty, and unknowns. Some changes surprise us and shake us out of our comfort zone, like losing a job, moving houses, or starting a new school. Some experiences change our reality drastically, such as being disappointed by mistakes made or losing a loved one. You might say surrendering is about putting aside what you think you need and asking God what He wants.

Surrender your life by walking in faith, not sight, and praying to God. When you pray, God enables you to surrender what you don't see and instead to see what God has for you, "as we look not to the things that are seen but to the things that are unseen. For the things that are seen are transient, but the things that are unseen are eternal" (2 Corinthians 4:18 ESV). You may know what you need to surrender, but it can be hard to let go. Don't be discouraged; one way to lean in is to cultivate the desire for God's presence until it is your deepest longing.

St. Francis of Assisi penned the words, "God, my God, I want to be filled with you." May these words be the cry of our own hearts!

2 Chronicles 7—Surrendered to God's Promise

When we surrender to God in the place of prayer, we also discover God, who is Yahweh - I AM. God demonstrates His power in our surrender. This verse in Chronicles is David's prayer for Solomon: "Then the Lord appeared to Solomon by night and said to him: I have heard your prayer and have chosen this place for Myself as a house of sacrifice" (2 Chronicles 7:12 NKJV).

In this passage, God displayed His authority to Solomon, His ability to give and take away. God has the ability to shut up Heaven, but the simple prayers of His people will bring restoration to their land. As God continued, "If My people who are called by My name will humble themselves, and pray, and seek My face, and turn from their wicked ways; then will I hear from heaven and I will forgive their sin, and I will heal their land" (2 Chronicles 7:14 NKJV).

It's hard to pray and be prideful.

Notice the keyword "IF." It's hard to pray and be prideful. I suppose you can, but if you would come before the Lord and place yourself on His spiritual MRI table and let Him examine your heart, you would probably find He's able to heal the parts of your heart you have tried to hide away.

Many of us can read the words of God in 2 Chronicles and see the mirror into our world. If the people of God today would do what this passage suggests—humble themselves, pray, and seek His face—God would forgive and heal the land as it was in the days of Solomon. That is the promise of God.

Surrender with Prayer—In Difficult Times

Surrender. It's a word that can strike fear into most people's hearts because they want control of their lives and to be the captain of their ship, even at the smallest level. But, we get the ultimate benefit when we allow God our Father to be at the ship's helm, navigating the rough waters with us.

We must remember that Jesus experienced the fullness of human emotion, including grief and despair. We see His humanity in the story of Lazarus. Jesus arrived in town to find His friend already dead in the tomb, leading us to the shortest yet one of the most profound verses in the Bible, which simply says "Jesus wept" (John 11:35 NKJV).

We have a Savior who is acquainted with our tears. In the Garden of Gethsemane, He felt the weight of anxiety so strongly that He began to sweat blood. He was so overwhelmed that He even asked God to remove His need to be sacrificed for us. And yet, Jesus knew the power of surrender and said, "Not My will, but Yours, be done" (Luke 22:42 NKJV). We rest in the fact that God knows intimately what it is like to be human, yet He knows how our story ends. After all, He is the author and finisher of our faith (Hebrews 12:2).

Pray that God will be honored and glorified, whatever your circumstance, even if you have to suffer or go through a difficult time. He instructs you to "call upon me in the day of trouble; I will deliver you, and you will honor me" (Psalms 50:15 NIV).

In times of prayer, God is there to support, encourage, and deliver you. It is implied that God will be right there, and we can call upon Him—"Because he has set his love upon Me, therefore I will deliver him; I will set him on high, because he has known My name. He shall call upon Me, and I will answer him; I will be with him in trouble; I will deliver him and honor him" (Psalms 91:14-15 NKJV).

NOT MY WILL, BUT YOURS BE DONE—A MESSAGE TO ALL WHO LONG TO LIVE A LIFE SURRENDERED TO PRAYER AND TO GOD'S WILL.

No human being who isn't acquainted with troubles is alive on this planet. Times of difficulty arrive unexpectedly and can remain indefinitely, and the sorrowful memories they produce take deep root in the mind. It is no wonder why Jesus' promise in John 16:33 talks to the hearts of so many Christians: "In this world you will have trouble. But take heart! I have overcome the world" (NIV).

Not my will, but yours be done—a message to all who long to live a life surrendered to prayer and to God's will.

When God's Yes is a No

The year was 2015. I was blessed to have been invited to preach in the southern part of Kenya, in a very remote area a couple of hours away from the Ugandan border. We had spent $45,000 for this crusade, hoping for a big turnout, and, as always, had planned for a three-day event.

On Friday night, we arrived at the crusade grounds to a glorious crowd of tens of thousands of people. The hunger for God was palpable. The worship team began to lead the crowd in song, and you could feel the presence of the Lord. The crusade director got up to introduce me just before we began the night.

About a minute or two after I began to speak, it started to drizzle. This was not in my plan, nor was it the rainy season. Immediately, I prayed, "Lord, stop the rain! I can't let these people leave without hearing Your Word!" I was afraid the rain would push people away. The rain, instead, picked up, but not a single person left the field. It continued to rain harder, and, as I was preaching, I began to think about how I needed to wrap up. I made the call to salvation, and every hand was raised. I was shocked, to say the least!

Still soaking wet, I got back to the hotel to find all these pastors waiting for me. They were dancing outside the hotel, some with great tears of joy. Confused, I asked, "What is going on?" I learned that it hadn't rained in that area for six months, the area so dry that the Kenyan people had to ration food for their children, their crops wouldn't grow, and the livestock was pencil-thin. They had desperately needed a miracle.

This happened for the next three days; it would rain through the night, the day would be clear, and after the worship team would sing, it would rain again while I preached. This was a sign to the people that God had heard their prayers. God's no to my prayers was instead a yes to theirs.

Grief and Surrender

It's easy to worship God when it seems as though your prayers are being answered, but what do you do when God does not give you what you pray for? Some people choose to walk away and deny His goodness as a result. But, in Scripture we see many examples of how grief and loss can be a catalyst to enter into the surrendered life.

Paul and Silas prayed for a slave girl to be set free from a demon in Acts 16, and as a result, they were beaten and thrown in prison. Doing the will of God caused them to suffer great pain. Nevertheless, they were secure in knowing that they had an Advocate, a Savior. They remembered the words of Jesus about two believers agreeing and praying in His name. In the midnight hour, they still had a fire burning on the inside of them to worship instead of complain. That still, small voice of God through the prophet Jeremiah could have sounded in their minds, saying, "Call to me and I will answer you" (Jeremiah 33:3 ESV). Paul and Silas called out to God, and boy, did He ever answer!

The first step is to ask yourself, "What do I need to surrender to God in this season of life?" For some, it could be a job, a relationship, or a burden you've been carrying. We serve a God who can shoulder the load. "Then Jesus said, 'Come to me, all you who are weary and burdened, and I will give you rest. Take my yoke upon you and learn from me, for I am gentle and humble in heart, and you will find rest for your souls.'" (Matthew 11:28-29 NIV).

God already knows what you're facing. He is simply asking you to let go of your burdens and place them in His hands. "Cast your burden upon the Lord, and He will sustain you; He will never allow the righteous to be shaken" (Psalms 55:22 NASB).

Grief is a part of life's challenges, and Jesus weeps with us in our grief, as it was with Mary and Martha because of the death of their brother Lazarus. Even though they were sisters and probably very similar to each other in many ways, Mary and Martha handled their brother's death very differently. Their different ways of dealing with Lazarus' death teach us important lessons about how Christians experience and deal with grief.

When their brother fell ill, Mary and Martha knew whom to call. The sisters sent a messenger to Jesus, saying, "'Lord, he whom you love is ill.' But when Jesus heard it, he said, 'This illness does not lead to death. It is for the glory of God, so that the Son of God may be glorified through it.' Now Jesus loved Martha and her sister and Lazarus. So, when he heard that Lazarus was ill, he stayed two days longer in the place where he was. Then after this, he said to the disciples, 'Let us go to Judea again'" (John 11:3-7 ESV).

The two sisters responded differently. As you might imagine, Martha expressed anger about her brother's death. When Jesus came to visit them after Lazarus had died, Martha said to Jesus, "Lord, if you had been here, my brother would not have died" (John 11:21 ESV). She was angry about her brother's death like many people would be, but Jesus was not frustrated with her. He understood that it is normal for us to feel angry when someone or something we love dies. God understands how we feel.

Mary reacted differently from Martha; she cried and wept. She may also have been angry, but she was mostly sad and depressed. "When Jesus saw her weeping, and the Jews who had come with her also weeping, he was deeply moved in his spirit and greatly troubled" (John11:33 ESV). God is not put off by our tears. After all, He is the one who gave us the ability to grieve.

Then Jesus, deeply moved again, came to the tomb. It was a cave, and a boulder lay against it. Jesus said, "Take away the stone." Mary and Martha didn't understand why Jesus would do this. But Jesus responded by reminding them of what he had said earlier, "Did I not tell you that if you believed, you would see the glory of God?" So, the sisters agreed, and they took away the stone. "And Jesus lifted his eyes and said, 'Father, I thank you that you have heard me. I knew that you always hear me, but I said this on account of the people standing around, that they may believe that you sent me.' When he had said these things, he cried out with a loud voice, 'Lazarus, come out'" (John 11:38-43 ESV).

Death can cause us to feel many different emotions. People react differently to death. Jesus did not condemn Martha's anger or Mary's sadness. Jesus wants us to know that He is always with us, comforting and assuring us whenever we experience grief.

Transition to Transformation—The Circle of Life

Sometimes, God brings times of transition to create transformation in life. Your life is a transition story, always leaving one chapter behind while moving on to the next. The story of David, the shepherd boy, transitioned to David, the king. The circle began with the life of Samuel. Samuel's mother Hannah, prayed to the Lord, saying:

"O Lord of hosts, if you will indeed look on the affliction of your servant and remember me and not forget your servant, but will give to your servant a son, then I will give him to the Lord all the days of his life" (1 Samuel 1:11 ESV). The Lord heard the depths of Hannah's prayer and showed Himself faithful by answering the cry of her heart. He gave her a little boy named Samuel, meaning, "Asked of God." This boy grew up to become one of the greatest prophets and priests the world has ever known, the one to give Israel their great king, David.

The people wanted Saul as the king, but Samuel sought another king to please God. The Lord said to Samuel: "How long will you grieve over Saul, since I have rejected him as king over Israel? Fill your horn with oil, and go. I will send you to Jesse the Bethlehemite, for I have provided for myself a king among his sons" (1 Samuel 16:1 ESV).

The Lord said to Samuel: "Do not look on his appearance or on the height of his stature, because I have rejected him. For the Lord sees not as man sees: man looks on the outward appearance, but the Lord looks on the heart" (1 Samuel 16:7 ESV). It seemed that Samuel would find a king for Israel in the house of Jesse's sons, but only David would be chosen.

"There remains yet the youngest," said Jesse, once Samuel and rejected all the other sons as God's chosen king. Jesse continued that "he is keeping the sheep." Samuel answered, "Send and get him, for we will not sit down till he comes here." Jesse's youngest son was then brought in. As soon as David walked in the room, the Lord said to Samuel: "Arise, anoint him, for this is he" (1 Samuel 16:11-12 ESV).

A judge became the greatest prophet in the history of Israel, and Samuel circled the path of life when David was chosen as king.

Psalm 139 is one of the most loved Psalms David ever wrote. It gives us a clear picture of the beauty of the all-knowing God:

"O Lord, you have searched me and known me! You know, when I sit down, and when I rise up, you discern my thoughts from afar. You search out my path and my lying down and are acquainted with all my ways. Even before a word is on my tongue, behold, O Lord, you know it altogether" (Psalms 139:1-4 ESV).

Serving the omniscient God should lead us to a place of peace. The psalm continues, "Before I formed you in your mother's womb, I knew you." God knows us better than we can know ourselves. Because He knows us so intimately and deeply, we should feel the security to run to Him no matter what, like a child running into a loving father's arms.

> **God knows us better than we can know ourselves. We should feel the security to run to Him no matter what.**

"Where shall I go from your Spirit? Or where shall I flee from your presence? If I ascend to heaven, you are there! If I make my bed in Sheol, you are there! If I take the wings of the morning and dwell in the uttermost parts of the sea, even there your hand shall lead me, and your right hand shall hold me" (Psalms 139:7-10 ESV).

God is present in every corner of the earth. All attempts to hide from the Lord are futile because He is everywhere. With this in mind, we can find in the life of surrender a glorious safe haven for all who have been wandering through the dark night of the soul. There is no space that His light is hidden from, no land that is without His presence, and no enemy that can derail you when your life is fully surrendered to Him.

Chapter Six

The Fuel For Evangelism

My spiritual father, Reinhard Bonnke, told the most incredible stories because he was a one-of-a-kind man. His testimony has impacted millions of people across the world. In his book, *Living a Life of Fire,* he retells the story of his encounter with the great evangelist George Jeffreys:

> I traveled by train to London…At length, I arrived at a place called Clapham Commons, a large park in a lovely residential section of the city. With no specific destination in mind, I decided to stretch my legs, and I began walking through the surrounding neighborhood totally at random. All of a sudden I stopped because I saw a blue nameplate in front of a house. On that nameplate I read, "George Jeffreys."
>
> I thought to myself, could this be the great George Jeffreys who had founded the Elim Pentecostal Churches in Ireland and England? I had read much about him. He had been a great firebrand evangelist who had traveled across the world preaching to overflow crowds in some of the largest venues. Miraculous signs and wonders had accompanied his preach-

ing. I recalled that 10,000 had been saved in his historic Birmingham crusade. 14,000 had responded during a crusade in Switzerland. He was known to many as the greatest evangelist Britain had produced after George Whitfield and John Wesley. My heart pounded with anticipation to think that of all the residences in London I might have stumbled upon, I had stumbled upon his.

I paused at the gate. Should I go in and introduce myself? I felt almost compelled to do it. But who was I to do such a thing?

I felt a spiritual and natural link with this man. As with so many other British revival leaders, Jeffreys had been born in Wales to a miner's family. He had been a teenager during the great Welsh Revival of 1904 and 1905, and for him, the fire had never gone out. What especially linked him to me was that he had also ridden the ride of the Pentecostal revival that followed from Azusa Street and onward. He had embraced both revivals.

You only live once, I decided. I walked through the front garden gate and climbed the porch, pausing at the door. There I rang the bell. A lady opened the door.

"Pardon my intrusion, ma'am. Does the George Jeffreys live here who was that famous firebrand evangelist I have heard so much about?"

"Yes, he does."

"May I please see him?"

"No. Under no circumstances."

She had hardly said no when I heard a deep voice from within the house say, "Let the young man come in."

I squeezed past that lady in a heartbeat and into the house. As my eyes adjusted to the dim light, I saw him coming slowly down a staircase, holding it unsteadily as he made his way toward me. As he reached the landing, I stepped forward, took his hand, and introduced myself. I told him I had a call of God on my life to be an evangelist and to preach the gospel in Africa. That I had been to college in Swansea and was now returning home to Germany.

What happened next was extraordinary. All of a sudden, he took me by the shoulders and fell to his knees, pulling me to the floor with him. He placed his hands on my head and began to bless me as a father blesses a son, as Abraham blessed Isaac, who blessed Jacob, and on and on. The room seemed to light up with the glory of God as he poured out his prayer over me. I was dazed by that glory. I do not remember the words with which he blessed me, but I do remember their effect. My body felt electrified, tingling with divine energy.

After about a half hour he finished. I stood up and helped him to his feet. He seemed very frail. We said goodbye. The lady came and escorted him away. He could hardly stand. Nor could I, for different reasons. I stumbled from his house and staggered back toward Clapham Commons like a drunken man. There, with my head spinning, I waited for a bus to carry me on my way to the railway station.

What were the odds that this had happened to me? Even more, what did it mean that it had happened to me? It seemed like a dream. I had to convince myself, again and again, that it had actually happened. Why would God grant me this unexpected and unplanned meeting as a 21-year-old Bible college graduate in London on his way home to serve a practicum at the smallest church in all of Germany?

I did not know. I kept it to myself.

I arrived at home and began the process of serving with my father in Krempe. I had been home for just a few months when one day Father said to me, "Son, did you hear the sad news?"

"No, what news?"

"George Jeffreys died in London."

"George Jeffreys! That's impossible, Father. I just saw him. I met him." And then I told him the story of my meeting with him in London.

In fact, he died on January 26, 1962. I was still 21, three months short of my 22nd birthday. As I absorbed the news, I realized something wonderful had happened in London. I had caught Elijah's mantel that day. God had connected me with former generations of evangelists - George Whitfeld, John Wesley, Evan Roberts, George Müller, Rees Howells, and George Jeffreys. The gospel is like a baton in a relay race and that day the baton was passed into my hands. The fire already blazed within me. The fire is always fresh, but the baton of the gospel is always old, as it is passed on from generation to generation. I now understood that on that day in London, the baron and the flame had met."[1]

What is an Evangelist?

The Greek word "euangelistēs" means a messenger of God and a preacher of the Gospel as mentioned in the Bible in Acts 21:8, Ephesians 4:11, and 2 Timothy 4:5.

Ephesians 4:11-13 expresses Christ's purpose of building up the body of Christ, "Christ himself gave the apostles, the prophets, the evangelists, the pastors and teachers, to equip his people for works of service, so that the body of Christ may be built up until we all reach unity in the faith and in the knowledge of the Son of God and become mature, attaining to the whole measure of the fullness of Christ" (NIV).

In Acts 21:8, we find Philip, the newly established evangelist. Additionally, Paul called Timothy up into the role of evangelist in 2 Timothy 4:5. The mantle of the evangelist was crucial to the new church.

---

1 Bonnke, R. (2019). Baton and Flame Meet. *In Living a Life of Fire: An Autobiography* (pp. 133–135). essay, Harvester Services Inc.

I believe we are all called to evangelism, even if we don't carry the official title of evangelist. The woman at the well is considered the first evangelist, telling her village after an encounter with Jesus, "He told me everything I ever did" (John 4:39 NIV).

Just as Jesus and His Father are One, they both shared the same vision, which is described in John 3:16-17: "For God so loved the world that He gave His only begotten Son, that whoever believes in Him should not perish but have everlasting life. For God did not send His Son into the world to condemn the world, but that the world through Him might be saved" (NKJV).

Jesus Himself elaborated by saying in Luke 19:10, "For the Son of Man came to seek and save the lost" (NIV). That was His greatest desire. In the same vein, in Luke 9:1-10, He called the disciples together, gave them power, and equipped them to go and tell. He was also about to go to many villages, preaching the Gospel and healing the sick. You may be thinking, of course, that's what the original twelve disciples signed up for. They had a special calling of an evangelist, just as Jesus did. Let me also enlighten you through the very next chapter. In Luke 10:1, Jesus called seventy others, men and women who were instructed to do the same thing. Ordinary, average people whose names are left in obscurity were also called to evangelism.

> **Evangelism was so embedded in Jesus' heart that in the most prominent years of his life, all He did was evangelize.**

Evangelism was so embedded in Jesus' heart that in the most prominent years of his life, all He did was evangelize. He didn't build a church, an orphanage, a ministry, a well. The only feeding program He put on was with the 5,000. He saw His time as so short that He spent His days focusing on two things: prayer and evangelism.

With this in mind, the early church took Christ at His word and obeyed the command of "go into all the world and preach the Gospel." They took this commission so seriously that it wound up costing them their lives. They never sat in one place; they evangelized the whole world.

Let me take a moment to introduce you to an individual who can get lost in Scripture. There are two Philips mentioned in the New Testament, but we'll focus on Philip the Evangelist. Also sometimes known as Philip the Deacon, he was chosen as one of the seven deacons to help the apostles on their mission of teaching and prayer (Acts 6:3).

The Gospel Preached in Samaria—"Those who had been scattered preached the word wherever they went. Philip went down to a city in Samaria and proclaimed the Messiah there. When the crowds heard Philip and saw the signs he performed, they all paid close attention to what he said. For with shrieks, impure spirits came out of many, and many who were paralyzed or lame were healed. So there was great joy in that city" (Acts 8:4-8 NIV). In the early church, evangelists went everywhere, preaching the Gospel and seeing people get saved, healed, and delivered.

Also in Acts 8, Philip first encountered a man named Simon, who was considered a magi, someone who did magic and divination through science in the ancient world. He claimed to be someone of godly authority, with crowds calling him "The Great Power of God" (Acts 8:10 NKJV).

Philip arrived on the scene and shared the Gospel with the crowds. After hearing his message, they began to believe and be baptized, including Simon! No power that is not of God can compare; the wizard was in awe of the signs and wonders that followed Philip wherever he went.

Philip Encountered the Ethiopian Eunuch—Philip's second notable experience of preaching the Gospel is chronicled later in the same chapter: "Now an angel of the Lord spoke to Philip, saying, 'Arise and go toward the south along the road which goes down from Jerusalem to Gaza.' This is desert. So he arose and went" (Acts 8:26-27 NKJV).

Philip encountered an Ethiopian man, who was a eunuch and an official for the queen of the Ethiopians. In his chariot, he was reading the Book of Isaiah, specifically Isaiah 53:7-8. "He was oppressed and He was afflicted, Yet He opened not His mouth; He was led as a lamb to the slaughter, And as a sheep, before its shearers is silent, So He opened not His mouth. He was taken from prison and from judgment, And who will declare His generation? For He was cut off from the land of the living; For the transgressions of My people He was stricken" (NKJV). The eunuch asked Philip to interpret the passage, which led Philip to evangelize by telling him about the Good News of Jesus and baptize him.

When they came out of the water, the Spirit of the Lord caught Philip away so that the eunuch saw him no more; and he went on his way rejoicing.

Jesus' Transition

After His death, burial, and resurrection, Jesus spent forty days with with disciples and others, encouraging them and preaching to them. Just before His ascension, Jesus told them to wait and pray in the upper room. For ten days, the disciples had a prayer meeting, waiting for the promises of Jesus. They didn't know what they were waiting for. They had a burning passion for evangelism, but Jesus said to wait.

First, pray. Prayer feeds the fires of evangelism. After they had spent ten days praying, they were filled with holy fire. The great Reinhard Bonnke used to say that "there is a flame for every name." Jesus wanted them to be filled with not only His passion but His power as well. That was the fuel for the birth of the new church. Before they became evangelists, they had to first be filled with His power.

As Isaiah said, "those who wait on the Lord Shall renew their strength" (Isaiah 40:31 NKJV). The greatest way to be inundated with God's power is to first pray. As the disciples learned firsthand from witnessing the daily life of Christ, the greatest way to be filled with His power is through living a life of prayer.

However, the disciples were left asking the same question you might find yourself asking, "Where do I start?" I can imagine the state of mind they must have been in. After being with Jesus physically for three years, they were on their own. The emotional and spiritual side of life they found themselves in must have been overwhelming. They probably found it very difficult to pray, just as Paul said to the Roman church, "For we do not know what we should pray for as we ought, but the Spirit Himself makes intercession for us with groanings which cannot be uttered." Even in a moment of great conflict, we have an Intercessor who spurs us on. Charles Spurgeon said, "Groanings which cannot be uttered are often prayers which cannot be refused."[2]

EVEN IN A MOMENT OF GREAT CONFLICT, WE HAVE AN INTERCESSOR WHO SPURS US ON.

We are not called to evangelize alone. Jesus gave us His Holy Spirit to empower and guide us to the people with whom we need to share the Gospel. We can rest in the fact that even if we don't have a spiritual mentor, we have the greatest Evangelist within reach. Every time you go to pray, it's like refueling your car, breath for your lungs, water for your body—fuel for your soul. The Spirit replenishes us so that we can go and tell.

Elijah passed the mantle to Elisha, Moses passed the mantle to Joshua, and Jesus passed the mantle to the disciples. We have all been given the mantle to share through the power of the Holy Spirit.

We see this model unfold in the New Testament church. Christ had made the truth known to Paul. Paul gave it to Timothy. Timothy was to pass it on to faithful men. These faithful men were to pass it on to others. There is an eternal lineage of faith in the family of God, and that includes every one of us.

Prayer for Effective Evangelism

As we've discussed in this book, prayer is one of the most powerful tools we have at our disposal. Jesus reminded us that "prayer moves mountains."

---

2 C. H. Spurgeon, *The Metropolitan Tabernacle Pulpit Volume 26: Sermons Preached and Revised in 1880* (London, England: Banner of Truth Trust, 1971).

The prayer of my life is that God would put someone in my path with whom to share the Good News. It doesn't matter if I'm on stage in front of 100,000 people, in an Uber, or sitting in a coffee shop. I see God's creations as His prized possessions, yet they are also lost, hurting, and confused people. We have the answer for hope and salvation!

God's design for His creation comes with specific purpose. God never intended that any living thing He created should just be born, live, and die. Jesus states that the two greatest commands are to love God and love your neighbor. If these are our main objectives, we must put a huge emphasis on bringing the treasure of the Gospel to our neighbors and beyond. That is love. If you had the cure for cancer but never told anyone, it would be the greatest crime humanity has ever seen. Yet we have the eternal cure for sin and death, and we fail to give it to our neighbors. The divine genius of God put the need for Him into His creation, but someone must tell them. Paul asks how people can know if they have not heard (Romans 10:14), and telling them is our responsibility. The greatest show of love for our neighbors is to share the opportunity for new life with them.

JESUS STATES THAT THE TWO GREATEST COMMANDS ARE TO LOVE GOD AND LOVE YOUR NEIGHBOR. IF THESE ARE OUR MAIN OBJECTIVES, WE MUST PUT A HUGE EMPHASIS ON BRINGING THE TREASURE OF THE GOSPEL TO OUR NEIGHBORS AND BEYOND. THAT IS LOVE.

Many Christians believe that the whole world has already heard the Gospel. That is simply not true. Oswald Smith says, "We talk of the Second Coming; half the world has never heard of the first."[3] According to The Joshua Project's latest statistics, nearly half of the

3 Oswald J. Smith, *The Challenge of Missions* (Waynesboro, GA: OM Literature, 1999).

world has not heard the Gospel, about 3.4 billion people. We travel the world to put on large Gospel Crusades, which we call Jesus Festivals, and we see this with our own eyes. There is still much work to be done in evangelism!

Jesus says the harvest is plentiful, and the laborers are few—"Therefore, pray the Lord of the harvest to send out laborers into His harvest" (Matthew 9:38 NKJV).

Notice that Jesus says PRAY to the Lord of the harvest. Prayer is the bedrock that fuels our evangelism efforts. We pray that God would lead us and guide us to whomever we need to reach, we pray He gives us the right words to say, and we pray that He gives us His heart for the lost. Without prayer, I believe our efforts to save souls are futile. It's like trying to start a car with no gas in the tank. Prayer to the Lord our God is the fuel that gives us the ability to operate, not in our own power, but in His.

PRAYER TO THE LORD OUR GOD IS THE FUEL THAT GIVES US THE ABILITY TO OPERATE, NOT IN OUR OWN POWER, BUT IN HIS.

Prayer, Evangelism, and Revival

In Mark 1, Peter told Jesus of his sick mother-in-law. Filled with compassion for His friend and family, Jesus prayed for the woman to be healed. Immediately, her fever broke and she served them in her home. This miracle caught the attention of the whole village. Before we know it, Scripture paints a beautiful picture of everyone in the city, all with various diseases, coming to get healed by Jesus! Wow! We know there's no sickness that He can't heal.

This pattern constantly repeated in the life of Christ! Pray, evangelize, and heal. In the very next section, as the disciples were still reeling with the Heavenly residue of what had taken place the night before, they were riding on clouds of joy. Yet they couldn't find Jesus. Where was He? Surely, after all that had happened the previous night, there was more to be done. They wanted to stay. They must have thought, we're just getting started! As they continued looking for their fearless leader, they finally found Him in a secluded place, talking to His Father.

Jesus said, "Let us go on to the next towns, that I may preach there also, for that is why I came out" (Mark 1:38 ESV). This is the way of Jesus: prayer first, then evangelism, then revival.

A Brief Glimpse Into The History of Revival

Revival is cross-denominational and transcendental. Around 300 years ago, The First Great Awakening took place throughout Britain and the original thirteen colonies, marking the emergence of a new kind of evangelism. The doctrine of the Reformation married with the power of the Holy Spirit and an emphatic kind of preaching set a new standard in the evangelical world. This movement birthed the legacy of George Whitefield, John Wesley, Jonathan Edwards, and others.

The Second Great Awakening moved the needle on the evangelical presence in the United States, spreading to over 1,500 towns in the infant country over forty years. There were many other revivals across the world and throughout history, but the Azusa Street Revival in 1906, helmed by William J. Seymour, led to the new Pentecostal and Charismatic movements. God began to move again in the mid-1990s, birthing the Toronto Blessing, the Melbourne Revival, the Modesto Revival, and the Brownsville Revival. God is not bound by geographical lines, for in 2001, in Lagos, Nigeria, the great Reinhard Bonnke saw millions of people gather and over 3.4 million people come to Christ in a single meeting.

As we peer through the window of time, God's desire to see His children saved still burns bright within Him; every tribe, tongue, and nation must be saved. What do these revivals have in common? Prayer and evangelism. God moved on people He found who were praying and evangelizing; these are the two threads woven together into His brilliant tapestry.

Chapter Seven

The Power and Purpose of Prayer

"No man is greater than his prayer life. The pastor who is not praying is playing; the people who are not praying are straying. We have many organizers, but few agonizers; many players and payers, few pray-ers; many singers, few clingers; lots of pastors, few wrestlers; many fears, few tears; much fashion, little passion; many interferers, few intercessors; many writers, but few fighters. Failing here, we fail everywhere."

—LEONARD RAVENHILL[4]

Many Christians believe that praying the Sinner's Prayer is all you need to do to live with God. After we pray, we're good. That's it. Let's move on. While believing and confessing that Jesus is Lord leads to everlasting life, it's simply the beginning, not the end. We don't have to wait to walk through those beautiful pearly gates in Heaven to experience

4 Leonard Ravenhill, *Why Revival Tarries* (Minneapolis, MN: Bethany House Publishers, 2004).

a passionate life with God our Father. He wants to commune with us here on earth daily and give us His power. He communicated with the disciples in Acts 1, commanding them to wait there until they were endowed with power from on high. After He gave that command, He ascended into Heaven, and over 500 people witnessed this glorious moment. Yet we find only 120 people in the upper room praying! They had prayed for ten days straight. Their hearts were set on obeying His command of waiting and praying, and praying and waiting. Then, and only then, would they experience the power of God in a tangible way. But where were the others? Over 380 people missed out on the Holy Spirit moving in on them like a rushing, mighty wind!

You must remember we serve the God who wants to give us "immeasurably more than all we ask or imagine, according to his power that is at work within us" (Ephesians 3:20 NIV). Every word that falls from our lips is received in the ears of God.

Power is the result of a consistent prayer life. Power accompanies prayer. When a man or woman sets their heart to pray, God sets His ears to hear. Not only to hear, but also to answer. Most of us grow impatient because we don't understand the discipline of waiting.

> **POWER IS THE RESULT OF A CONSISTENT PRAYER LIFE. POWER ACCOMPANIES PRAYER. WHEN A MAN OR WOMAN SETS THEIR HEART TO PRAY, GOD SETS HIS EARS TO HEAR. NOT ONLY TO HEAR, BUT ALSO TO ANSWER.**

Jesus said persistence is vital. Even an unjust judge was gracious to grant the requests of a persistent widow (Luke 18). The judge was not even godly; how much more will your Heavenly Father grant your requests? The Lord is a thousand times longing to hear us and a thousand and one times ready to answer, but we quickly and easily give up asking. We don't know what it means to wait. However, just as Isaiah 40:31 says, they that wait on the Lord will have their strength renewed.

The Power of Prayer in Acts

After this heavenly encounter with the Holy Spirit and the forming of the church, as a result of the disciples' prayer meeting, three thousand people came to a place of full surrender to Christ! Three thousand people were saved in the very first meeting. Then, the disciples went back to pray. Shortly after, we read the record of five thousand men being saved in Acts 2, not counting women and children.

Prayer is the fuel that gives us the power to accomplish the things God sets before us. It is helpful to the believer's life and essential to see His Kingdom come here and now.

> PRAYER IS THE FUEL THAT GIVES US THE POWER TO ACCOMPLISH THE THINGS GOD SETS BEFORE US.

The power of a prayer life is evident to even the unbeliever. Once the people on the streets heard the disciples speaking in tongues in Acts 4, they were amazed, and this gave Peter an opening to address them. They were cut to the heart and said to Peter and the other apostles, "Brothers, what shall we do?" Peter replied, "Repent and be baptized, every one of you, in the name of Jesus Christ for the forgiveness of your sins. And you will receive the gift of the Holy Spirit." The result was revival. "And they devoted themselves to the apostles' teaching and the fellowship, to the breaking of bread and the prayers" (Acts 2:37-38,42 ESV).

Prayer did not stop after that experience at Pentecost. It was just the beginning. As Leonard Ravenhill said, "A man who is intimate with God is not intimidated by man."[5] The disciples lived this life of boldness. We can also see this experience in our lives. The more intimate we are with God, the more God will clothe us with fearlessness. The disciples' only objective was to please the One who gave His life for them. Our objective is the same; we want to give our lives to the One who gave all for us.

---

5 Leonard Ravenhill, *Meat for Men* (Pensacola, FL: Christian Life Books, 2008).

The disciples felt so convicted about this newfound love of prayer that they said in Acts 6:4 that their greatest responsibility was to devote themselves to prayer first and then the ministry of the Word. My personal prayer is that while you're reading this, you, too, discover that one of your most significant responsibilities is to spend time with the Heavenly Father in prayer.

In Acts 10, a man named Cornelius, who happened to be a Roman military official, was a leader in the region of Judea. Most Romans of that time believed in many unique gods—but he was different. He feared the one true God. We read that he was a man of prayer who also gave generously to the poor and needy (Acts 10:2).

Unfortunately for Cornelius, the Jewish people simply would not accept him as one of their own due to nationality. Still, God recognized him as one of His own. Cornelius was in complete agreement with God about what was good. Therefore, he acted accordingly.

Because of Cornelius' devotion to prayer, God chose him for a particular assignment and sent an angel— "About the ninth hour of the day, he saw clearly in a vision an angel of God come in and say to him, 'Cornelius.' And he stared at him in terror and said, 'What is it, Lord?' And he said to him, 'Your prayers and your alms have ascended as a memorial before God'" (Acts 10:3-4 ESV).

Peter also heard from the Lord. He went up on the rooftop around the sixth hour to pray and fell into a trance. In that trance, three times God encouraged Peter to break the Jewish law of eating unclean food. Then, Cornelius' men sent for Peter. The first thing Peter asked was, "Why am I here?" Cornelius answered him, "Four days ago, about this hour, I was praying in my house at the ninth hour, and behold, a man stood before me in bright clothing and said, 'Cornelius, your prayer has been heard, and your alms have been remembered before God'" (Acts 10:30-31 ESV).

This is a pattern in the book of Acts: The disciples prayed, power was released, and they traveled on despite tremendous persecution and opposition. In Acts 16, as Paul, Timothy, and Silas headed to Philippi, they weren't looking for nice hotels, restaurants, the latest and greatest shopping centers, or a cool cafe; their main priority was looking for a place to pray. Many of us look for a city's main attractions when we travel. Not these guys; they were looking for an encounter with the Living God. And, because of their prayer, they encountered Lydia, who was baptized and invited the three of them to come to her home, where Paul later planted a thriving church.

Jesus Teaches on Prayer

Jesus often talked to the disciples about the importance of spending time in prayer. They witnessed the power of His prayer life, so much so that, as we have previously learned, it is one of the few questions recorded from the disciples to Jesus (Matthew 6:9-13).

The disciples learned how to pray through the teaching of Jesus. One day, Jesus was praying, and when he finished talking, one of his disciples said to him, "Lord, teach us to pray, as John also taught his disciples" (Luke 11:1 NKJV).

Jesus said, "When you pray, you shall not be like the hypocrites. For they love to pray standing in the synagogues and on the corners of the streets, that they may be seen by men. But you, when you pray, go into your room, and when you have shut your door, pray to your Father who is in the secret place; and your Father who sees in secret will reward you openly" (Matthew 6:5-6 NKJV).

Imagine sitting at the feet of the great intercessor Jesus and hearing Him tell us how to pray! It is a priceless opportunity to pass on to the disciples of the next generation. Remember that the Greek "proseúchomai" is always used for prayer to God and is the most frequent word used in this respect, especially in the Synoptic Gospels and Acts.

Imagine with me that we're gathered together in the church, and from the side of the stage, we catch a glimpse of a Pharisee, perhaps a scholar or leader in the community, and he walks up on stage, grabs the mic, and begins to pray the most eloquent and polished prayer all who sit in the congregation have ever heard. He mixes his prayer with some self-righteous accomplishments and a few Scriptures to make it seem like he's somebody you should be impressed with. All are awed by his knowledge of Scripture and use of the English language. Then, knowing he's done well, he receives the applause of men. He turns, places the mic down, and takes his seat. He sits there with somewhat of a pompous attitude. The only problem is, he's completely missed out on the applause of Heaven! His Heavenly Father has not received his pitiful prayer. After all, his prayer had a stench of pride attached to it when the Heavenly Father desires to have brokenness poured over it.

Jesus countered the religious pretenders of praying by instructing that when you pray, you should go to your room in the most secret place. The focus is on the intimacy of communion with God in one's heart, which is at the center of all prayer. In the secret place, you'll discover that private prayer alone with God is one of the best indicators of one's devotion to Christ because there is no one present to be impressed by your words except Jesus and the Holy Spirit, who give life to your prayers.

Purpose, Priority, and Position

Mary realized that her greatest purpose was to be with Him - to listen, to learn, and ultimately, to love Him deeply. She made being with Him her greatest priority. While her sister Martha was busy trying to entertain everyone, Mary was busy trying to love Him.

We see that because Mary had *purposed* in her heart to make being with Him her greatest *priority*, she *positioned* herself to quietly sit at His feet and listen to every word that dripped from His holy lips, for she knew He was truly Heaven's greatest treasure to mankind!

"Now it happened as they went that He entered a certain village; and a certain woman named Martha welcomed Him into her house. And she had a sister called Mary, who also sat at Jesus' feet and heard His word. But Martha was distracted with much serving, and she approached Him and said, 'Lord, do You not care that my sister has left me to serve alone? Therefore tell her to help me." And Jesus answered and said to her, 'Martha, Martha, you are worried and troubled about many things. But one thing is needed, and Mary has chosen that good part, which will not be taken away from her'" (Luke 10:38-42 NKJV).

Most of us can relate to one of these two sisters. They both loved Jesus but had vastly different approaches to display it. To Mary, she knew her rightful place was simply sitting at Jesus' glorious feet and loving Him with a love that she had never poured out on anyone. He was special to her and meant the world to her. She couldn't explain it - words didn't do justice to how she felt about Him, so she sat in holy awe. She sat in silence and just listened to God's One and only Son speak words of life.

Meanwhile, in the midst of the holy chaos, her sister Martha was concerned with all the people that had crashed her home. She wanted to be a good host. After all, she had a very important guest sitting in her little Jewish living room. For Martha, this was their home, their sanctuary, and like most of us, she wanted to make sure everyone was well taken care of. But in the hustle and bustle of this special moment, she noticed her sister did not help. Not only not helping, but she was sitting with the rest of the guests, listening to Jesus. The scripture says she positioned herself to be the closest to Him and sit at His feet. Mary wasn't concerned about the needs of the guests in her home; she was overwhelmed with the only Guest that truly mattered. She also knew that He wouldn't be in her living room for long, so she capitalized on every second He was there with her.

This obviously perturbed her sister Martha. Some would agree, maybe it was just to much for Martha to handle alone. Maybe you would agree that Mary should've been more aware of the moment and lent her sister a helping hand. But therein lies Mary's greatest attribute - she was more aware of the moment than her sister Martha. For Mary may have thought, "How could anyone possibly strive to host friends and family whom we have with us everyday, when the Son of God, our very Creator, humanity's loving Savior is here! How could anyone miss this Heavenly moment by entertaining everyone other than Him?"

> **When we set our hearts to pray, He sets His heart to come and be with us! When we position ourselves at His feet, we realize our purpose is to listen and pray.**

This is like the breath of prayer. The Lord desires to be with us way more then we desire to be with Him. When Martha went to Jesus to tell her sister Mary to help her out with her work load, Jesus lovingly corrected Martha and said (in our modern language), "Martha, you are worried about so many meaningless things, but your sister Mary chose the most important thing of all: sitting here with Me. That will never be taken from her."

Mary had set her heart to be with Him and we should do the same. When we set our hearts to pray, He sets His heart to come and be with us! When we position ourselves at His feet, we realize our purpose is to listen and pray. His glorious presence and power is the outcome.

Chapter Eight

Prayer and Intercession

"We never know how God will answer our prayers, but we can expect that He will get us involved in His plan for the answer. If we are true intercessors, we must be ready to take part in God's work on behalf of the people for whom we pray."
—Corrie ten Boom

Intercessory prayer is the standing in the gap we find in Ezekiel 22:30: "I searched for a man among them who would build up the wall and stand in the gap" (NASB).

Intercession means elevating the needs and anxieties of others to God, demonstrating selfless love. It is vital to pray for another, but there are times when someone prays for people without their knowledge, simply to encourage and support them through prayer.

The Greek word "enteuxis" means intercession, prayer petition, and supplication. The root of this word is "tugchanó," which means to hit, hit upon, meet, or happen. In the HELPS Word-Studies, "tugchanó" means to "become ready"—properly, to strike (hit the mark, i.e., "spot on," "hit the mark, "spot on," "hit the bullseye." Intercession leads us to hit our target head-on and aim for our prayers to be answered accurately.

Again, we need not look any further than Jesus to see this spirit of prayer and intercession fully displayed. He prayed for His followers during His life on earth and continued to petition the Father on our behalf.

Prayer is the most important thing you can do for another. The Apostle Paul wrote to the Roman church: "Likewise the Spirit also helps in our weaknesses. For we do not know what we should pray for as we ought, but the Spirit Himself makes intercession for us with groanings which cannot be uttered" (Romans 8:26-28 NKJV).

If the Spirit continually makes intercession for us, then we who know how to pray should also be making intercession for others. Every serious intercessor knows that the Lord does not wait for us to get ready when the time comes. Opportunity, after all, favors the prepared.

Intercession begins with God, the original motivator, who is always aware of the situation and will be the supporter and mediator in prayer. For those passionate about intercession for others, it is equivalent to what water is for human life; it quickly becomes a vital part of prayer.

FOR THOSE PASSIONATE ABOUT INTERCESSION FOR OTHERS, IT IS EQUIVALENT TO WHAT WATER IS FOR HUMAN LIFE; IT QUICKLY BECOMES A VITAL PART OF PRAYER.

Intercessory prayer births a great desire from God for others. Of course, we also pray for our own situations, but sometimes it is vital to intercede for others. Those moments are when you pray for someone without their knowledge, simply sensing something. An intercessor will be there to encourage and support someone in their prayers, even if they do not have all the details.

Throughout the Old Testament, God was open to the work of intercessors. Prophets like Moses, Jeremiah, and Ezekiel brought the Word of God from God to the people. Priests represented the people by coming before God's presence, as it was with Samuel being an intercessor for David.

As displayed in the New Testament, Christ is the ultimate intercessor. Because of this, we see that prayer, which comes from the child of God, becomes intercession since it is offered to God through Jesus! Jesus, on the other hand, because He continues forever, holds His priesthood permanently. "Therefore He is able also to save forever those who draw near to God through Him since He always lives to make intercession for them" (Hebrews 7:24-25 NASB).

Jesus built an eternal bridge from earth to Heaven when He died a horrific death on the cross. Because Jesus took our place and was our mediator, we can indeed intercede for others. Let's stand in the gap for our brothers and sisters in Christ and those far away from our Savior. "For there is one God and one Mediator between God and men, the Man Christ Jesus" (1 Timothy 2:5 NKJV).

First John 2:1 describes Jesus as an advocate: "My little children, these things I write to you, so that you may not sin. And if anyone sins, we have an Advocate with the Father, Jesus Christ the righteous" (NKJV). Only God can forgive sin, and though we have no claim on Him, the Intercessor can plead our case. The Bible uses many words for the Holy Spirit, as He is our Advocate. In other parts of the New Testament, He is our "Comforter"— "And I will ask the Father, and he will give you another Helper, to be with you forever, even the Spirit of truth" (John 14:16-17a ESV). Jesus is always advocating before the Father like a lawyer on our behalf. When Jesus ascended, He became and will always be humanity's great advocate. He does this because of man's special design, as we are the only created beings that are made in the image of God. "For we are His workmanship, created in Christ Jesus for good works, which God prepared beforehand so that we would walk in them" (Ephesians 2:10 NASB).

Christ the Mediator

The message is that Christ is the foundation of intercessory prayer. In New Testament Scriptures, our Lord Jesus Christ is called a mediator in several places. In Greek, that would be "mesitēs," the mediator or arbitrator. He's called a mediator in several ways, like someone who goes between for someone needing help.

The term "intercessor" occurs only once in the Bible. "He saw that there was no man, And wondered that there was no intercessor; Therefore His own arm brought salvation for Him; And His own righteousness, it sustained Him." (Isaiah 59:16 NKJV).

Even when the noun "intercessor" is not used, the expression "to make intercession" is sometimes used. The thought exists throughout Scripture. The verb "entynchanein" means to make intercession, to act as an inter-mediator.[6]

"Who then is the one who condemns? No one. Christ Jesus who died—more than that, who was raised to life—is at the right hand of God and is also interceding for us" (Romans 8:34 NIV).

> Jesus is the doorway that allows us open access to our Heavenly Father. Prayer is the key that opens or unlocks the door to our Heavenly Father.

Jesus is the doorway that allows us open access to our Heavenly Father. Prayer is the key that opens or unlocks the door to our Heavenly Father. Meanwhile, Jesus is continually, twenty-four hours a day, seven days a week, making intercession for us. That should bring us great comfort. The Alpha and the Omega, the Beginning and the End, the First and the Last, the Author and the Finisher of our faith, is interceding for us. So, we can draw closer to the Lord each day as we pray for others. To intercede with God is to pray fervently for others through the Holy Spirit. "But you, beloved,

6 James Strong, *Strong's Expanded Exhaustive Concordance of the Bible* (Nashville: Thomas Nelson, 2009), 1793.

building yourselves up on your most holy faith, praying in the Holy Spirit" (Jude 1:20 NKJV). We must also understand that God is there, if only we will ask. "Ask, and it will be given to you; seek, and you will find; knock, and it will be opened to you" (Matthew 7:7 NKJV).

The Call to Intercession and Prayer

This is a proclamation call to the body of Christ, a presentation of intercession to the new believer, and a refresher course to the intercessor. This is a challenge to be the person for whom God is always searching in these last days.

Our prayers make a wall or cause us to stand in the gap for others. Psalm 106:23 demonstrates the power of an Old Testament intercessor. "Therefore He said that He would destroy them, Had not Moses His chosen one stood before Him in the breach, To turn away His wrath, lest He destroy them" (NKJV). Intercession is not always easy because the people we are trying to intercede for the most are typically battling sin or blinded to the truth, just as Moses faced with the Israelites in the wilderness. But we can never give up praying, as God is always there to strengthen His people.

The Father is the one who hears, receives, and answers our prayers. He is the One intimately involved with the intercession process. After all, if it weren't for the love of the Father, we would not be able to pray at all. Prayer comes from the Father, and the Father is involved in intercession in many ways. As we know, the Lord is a gentleman. He doesn't force His way into our lives; rather, He knocks, just as John wrote in Revelation 3:20. "Behold, I stand at the door and knock" (NKJV). If someone listens to His voice and opens, He will come in and fellowship with them. Look closely at what the Lord says. He knocks and patiently waits for someone to answer. If you answer, He'll come in and fellowship with you; He won't leave. He stays!

HE KNOCKS AND PATIENTLY WAITS FOR SOMEONE TO ANSWER. IF YOU ANSWER, HE'LL COME IN AND FELLOWSHIP WITH YOU; HE WON'T LEAVE. HE STAYS!

Here is the work of the mediator and intercessor. An intercessor only prays and petitions, while a mediator guarantees to take responsibility. Christ is our intercessor through His relationship with the Father. He is our mediator through His atonement, by which He takes upon Himself the sins of all who are truly penitent. "For there is one God and one mediator between God and mankind, the man Christ Jesus," (1 Timothy 2:5 NIV). Therefore, He is able. As He ever lives, and ever intercedes, He has the power to save. Hebrews 7:25-26 says that He can save those who come to God through Jesus' intercession as a priest of the Most High through eternity.

Keys to Interceding with Influence

One of the keys to interceding with influence is to speak God's Word according to the situation. Psalm 138:2 says: "I will worship toward Your holy temple, And praise Your name for Your lovingkindness and Your truth; For You have magnified Your word above all Your name" (NKJV). When we neglect the Word of God, we ignore the very thing that can change people's lives. The Word of God can convict us of sin, teach us truth, and lead us in righteousness.

When praying, we must be led by listening to the Holy Spirit, our inner witness. God's Word is clear that the condition of your heart is critical in your walk with the Lord. "Above all else, guard your heart, for everything you do flows from it" (Proverbs 4:23 NIV).

Another way to intercede is through fasting and prayer. Fasting is abstaining significantly from food and routine activities to focus on God and on people who need our prayers. Moses fasted during the forty days and forty nights he was on Mount Sinai to receive the law from God. David fasted when he knew Saul and Jonathan had been killed (2 Samuel 1:12). Nehemiah prayed and fasted when he heard Jerusalem was in ruins (Nehemiah 1:4).

The heart is the gatekeeper of intercession through the voice of God. That beautiful inner voice guides us. With His voice, our inner witness, and this blueprint, we will surely not stray from the Lord's will. That inner witness comes from God, not from another source.

God showed Abraham this very way. "I am with you and will watch over you wherever you go, and I will bring you back to this land. I will not leave you until I have done what I have promised you" (Genesis 28:15 NIV). Peace is the voice of the inner witness; listen to it. Psalm 46:10: "Be still and know that I am God" (NIV). There is an art to being still and listening before the Lord. We've become so busy with life that we've forgotten the simplicity of turning our ears to His quiet, small voice.

The Intercessor Who Made a Prophet

One of the most incredible things you can ever do is to develop a ministry of prayer. Remember the deep pain and anguish that Hannah went through because she couldn't have children? She experienced the daily pain of seeing others close to her giving birth to their children, but the righteous Hannah was barren. She fell into deep sadness, possibly even depression, and then she turned to the Lord and poured her broken and bitter heart into prayer.

> "Now Eli the priest was sitting on his chair by the doorpost of the Lord's house. In her deep anguish Hannah prayed to the Lord, weeping bitterly. And she made a vow, saying, 'Lord Almighty, if you will only look on your servant's misery and remember me, and not forget your servant but give her a son, then I will give him to the Lord for all the days of his life, and no razor will ever be used on his head.'
>
> "As she kept praying to the Lord, Eli observed her mouth. Hannah prayed in her heart, and her lips moved, but her voice was not heard. Eli thought she was drunk and said, 'How long are you going to stay drunk? Put away your wine.'
>
> "'Not so, my lord,' Hannah replied. 'I am a woman who is deeply troubled. I have not been drinking wine or beer; I was pouring out my soul to the Lord. Do not take your servant for a wicked woman; I have been praying here out of my great anguish and grief.' Eli answered, 'Go in peace, and may the God of Israel grant you what you have asked of him.' She said, 'May

your servant find favor in your eyes.' Then she went her way and ate something, and her face was no longer downcast" (1 Samuel 1:9-18 NIV).

This is the story of the birth of an intercessor. In the old days, barrenness was considered almost the ultimate curse for a married woman. The main hope for women was that they could give their husband a son who would inherit their name. When Hannah found she was barren, she was very troubled and made it a point to continuously believe and pray. God answered her prayer, and Hannah, an intercessor, had a son. Her son, Samuel, became the greatest prophet and judge in all of Israel's history.

Intercessors Have God's Heart

"He saw that there was no man and wondered that there was no one to intercede; then his own arm brought him salvation, and his righteousness upheld him" (Isaiah 59:16 ESV). God looks for those whose hearts are ready to be intercessors before Him. The most effective intercessors must have hearts aligned with God's heart. They are so attuned to what is at stake for their ground that they will stay before God as long as needed to obtain God's answer. That is why you do not volunteer to be an intercessor. God enlists you.

The most effective intercessors must have hearts aligned with God's heart. That is why you do not volunteer to be an intercessor. God enlists you.

Many are gifted and passionate intercessors, but others are insecure and don't have the heart of intercession yet. The Apostle Paul was eager to encourage people to become intercessors. "I urge that supplications, prayers, intercessions, and thanksgivings be made for all people" (1 Timothy 2:1 ESV).

Prayer and intercession have a lot in common, and they often overlap one another. Many Christians are confused about the difference between prayer and intercession. Yet, in the teaching of Christ in John 15, in the testimony of the apostles, and in the lives of the prophets, it is clear!

When we pray, the emphasis is on "we" or "I" going to prayer! It is our prayer, or my prayer and desire. When we pray, we hope God will answer, and we hope our prayer is according to His will. However, in intercession, the Holy Spirit prays and intercedes. The intercessor only prays what the Holy Spirit asks them to plead.

Prayer often begins with us, but intercession must begin with the Holy Spirit. He tells the intercessor to pray for whatever matters, and the Holy Spirit directs the intercession. The Scriptures clarify that the Spirit and intercessors are joined as one. "God has given us his Spirit. This is how we know we are one with him, just as he is one with us" (1 John 4:13 CEV).

Scripture says we come to God's throne of grace boldly, and now we have the privilege of interceding for others through the power of the Holy Spirit. "Likewise the Spirit also helps in our weaknesses. For we do not know what we should pray for as we ought, but the Spirit Himself makes intercession for us with groanings which cannot be uttered. Now He who searches the hearts knows what the mind of the Spirit is, because He makes intercession for the saints according to the will of God" (Romans 8:26-27 NKJV).

Evangelism and Discipleship—Prayer and Intercession

Evangelism and discipleship, with prayer and intercession, are a perfect concoction for living a life with Christ. You have evangelism, or soul winning. This then leads to discipleship, growing daily in your walk with the Lord. Then you develop a practice of prayer, continually communicating with your Heavenly Father, and finally continuous prayer leads to intercession. It makes sense that every disciple should be committed to evangelism. The perspective of these four facets of life with Christ is seen in Matthew, the Book of Acts, and Ephesians.

"Go therefore and make disciples of all nations, baptizing them in the name of the Father and of the Son and of the Holy Spirit, teaching them to observe all that I have commanded you. And behold, I am with you always, to the end of the age" (Matt. 28:19-20 ESV). Growing disciples is part of the four keys to changing the culture. It requires a commitment to this cause because it is possible for the great commission to sadly become the great omission. This is why making disciples is so crucial.

Raising up Evangelists—As we see in Luke 10:1, the Lord sends out seventy others also, ordinary men and women like you and me, to go into every city, town, and village He was about to go into, and He instructed them to go and preach the Gospel. In order to do this effectively, He equipped them with the power to heal the sick, cast out demons, and set the oppressed free.

Jesus also displayed this in His ministry: "And Jesus went throughout all the cities and villages, teaching in their synagogues and proclaiming the gospel of the kingdom and healing every disease and every affliction and heal the sick there, and say to them, 'The kingdom of God has come near to you" (Matthew 9:1, 9, 11 ESV).

"Then those who gladly received His word were baptized, and that day, about three thousand souls were added to them. And they continued steadfastly in the apostles' doctrine and fellowship, in the breaking of bread, and in prayers and praising God and having favor with all the people. And the Lord added to the church daily those who were being saved" (Acts 2:41-42,47 NKJV). These verses focus on the training of disciples and evangelism, but what about prayers and intercession?

The church went into a season of intense intercession, bringing in strangers and foreigners to become citizens with the saints. Ephesians 2:17-19 says, "And He came and preached peace to you who were afar off and to those who were near. For through Him, we both have access by one Spirit to the Father. Now, therefore, you are no longer strangers and foreigners but fellow citizens with the saints and members of the household of God" (NKJV).

As indicated in Ephesians, Paul was a dominant intercessor who prayed constantly. "For this reason, I bow my knees to the Father of our Lord Jesus Christ, from whom the whole family in heaven and earth is named" (Ephesians 3:14-15 NKJV). As we reflect on the life of Paul, we can clearly see that he was not only a man of prayer, but his prayer life often led him to a place of intercession.

The Mystery of Intercession

There is a mysterious reason for the prophetic word in 1 Samuel: "So Samuel called to the Lord, and the Lord sent thunder and rain that day; and all the people greatly feared the Lord and Samuel (1 Samuel 12:18 NKJV). Samuel called; God answered. Again, we see this great man of prayer and intercession who has the ear of the Lord because God has his heart.

The signs stimulated Israel to seek Samuel's intercession: "Pray for your servants to the Lord your God, that we may not die; for we have added to all our sins the evil of asking for a king for ourselves" (1 Samuel 12:19 NKJV). Israel was well aware of their egregious sin. They ultimately rejected the Lord as their king and asked for a king they could physically see and talk to, yet they had the audacity to call themselves servants!

In a marvelous manifestation of the grace of God, Samuel's intercession for the people led to assurance that God would bless them despite their wrong choices. However, he said, they must be steadfast in their obedience from that point on. The past could not be undone, but their future was assured if they could be devoted to the Lord of Israel.

"And Samuel said to the people, 'Do not be afraid; you have done all this evil. Yet do not turn aside from following the Lord, but serve the Lord with all your heart. And do not turn aside after empty things that cannot profit or deliver, for they are empty. For his great name's sake, the Lord will not forsake his people because it has pleased the Lord to make you a people for himself'" (1 Samuel 12:20-22 ESV). The intercession brought them back to God, healed the nation, and prevented God's judgment for rejecting Him. Their hearts were now wide open to the Lord. They were clothed in repentance and brokenness.

"If my people who are called by my name humble themselves, and pray and seek my face and turn from their wicked ways, then I will hear from heaven and will forgive their sin and heal their land. Now my eyes will be open and my ears attentive to the prayer that is made in this place" (2 Chronicles 7:14-15 ESV).

Chapter Nine

Cultivating a Life of Prayer

"I tell you the truth, unless a kernel of wheat is planted in the soil and dies, it remains alone. But its death will produce many new kernels—a plentiful harvest of new lives. Those who love their life in this world will lose it. Those who care nothing for their life in this world will keep it for eternity."
(John 12:24-25 NLT)

As a seed is planted in seclusion, work begins to take place, unknown to the outer world, waiting to be revealed in due time. In the same way, we cultivate a life of prayer. We enter a secluded and private place, and God begins to do a work in us first. In His timing, He will publicly reveal what has been done in us privately.

Cultivating Humility

"Indeed, I count everything as loss because of the surpassing worth of knowing Christ Jesus my Lord. For his sake I have suffered the loss of all things and count them as rubbish, in order that I may gain Christ" (Philippians 3:8 ESV).

One day, while I was traveling with Pastor Bonnke, we headed back to our hotel after leaving a very important meeting with several of the most influential Christian leaders from all different parts of the world. I was slightly overwhelmed with a tremendous amount of gratitude. Maybe I was in awe of what had just taken place. I had been seated at a table next to Pastor Bonnke as several tremendous men of God fired questions at him. He graciously and effectively shared about the Great Commission and global evangelism for about one and a half hours. I could tell by looking at their faces that they, too, were in awe, for many of them viewed him as a spiritual hero. When we got back to our hotel later that afternoon, we sat down and had dinner. "Pastor Bonnke, I have to ask you this question. I've been thinking about this all afternoon after leaving the lunch meeting with all those great men earlier today. The way they listened intently to everything you said was somewhat astounding to me. But my question is, how do you not let it get to your head? I mean, after all, you are a human as well." He graciously looked at me without hesitation and said, "Bernie, it's very easy. Years ago, the Lord spoke to me and said, 'Reinhard, always stay on your knees, and people's praises will fly right over your head, just as well as their criticisms.'"

A Deeper Intimacy with God the Father

"For this reason I bow my knees before the Father, from whom every family in heaven and on earth is named, that according to the riches of his glory he may grant you to be strengthened with power through his Spirit in your inner being, so that Christ may dwell in your hearts through faith—that you, being rooted and grounded in love . . ." (Ephesians 3:14-17 ESV).

When we pray, we are not shouting into the void but speaking to a Person.

When we pray, we are not shouting into the void but speaking to a Person. Not just any person, but someone intimately acquainted with the intricacies of life.

Not just any person, but someone intimately acquainted with the intricacies of life. He is our Heavenly Father; He is our Creator. As he told the prophet Jeremiah, "I knew you before I formed you in your mother's womb," and, "Before you were born I set you apart" (Jeremiah 1:5 NLT). Therefore, we can take heart that He hears us and truly understands the daily struggles we face.

In Ephesians 3, Paul found himself upon his knees before God. In verse 12, he proclaimed, "in whom we have boldness and confidence through faith in Him" (NKJV). Our access to God is just a whisper away. God is worthy to be praised because He is the Author of the Universe and yet closer than a brother to those who call upon His name. Paul says again in Philippians 3:10, "that I may know Him and the power of His resurrection" (NKJV). His heart's cry was that we may know the living God!

In the Old Testament, no instance is described in which an individual prayed to God as his Father individually, but in Luke 11:2, Jesus told His followers, when you pray, say, "Father." We have the right to call upon God as our Father. In Ephesians 3, Paul still lived in the newness and uniqueness of saying "Father." And we should never lose the force of getting on our knees and calling God in Heaven Father, which should always leave us breathless. If God is our Father, we receive His power, possessions, concern, and love. Once your heart has been tuned to God's love, it sets you free to cultivate your life through a new way of praying.

Riches of His Glory—Power of His Spirit

Psalm 8 asks, "What is man that you are mindful of him, and the son of man that you care for him? Yet you have made him a little lower than the heavenly beings and crowned him with glory and honor. You have given him dominion over the works of your hands; you have put all things under his feet" (Psalm 8:4-6 ESV).

Israel's greatest king, King David, wrote in Psalm 139 about the wondrous intimacy with God he experienced. He said that this knowledge was too hard for him to understand! I can't help but think to myself, I wonder if David thought, you know, I'm a fairly intelligent individual; after all, Solomon came from my loins, but this kind of knowledge is still too overwhelming for me.

The whole concept is about really getting to know the Father. When we read Psalm 139, we know just how intimately the God of the Universe knows us. We desire the same thing these great men of old prayed for. Abraham was called the friend of God. How do you become a friend of God? By spending a lot of time talking to Him, listening to Him, and spending daily time getting to know Him and His ways. Our objective or desire when we pray is to be a friend of God. We then can know the vastness of the riches of His glory. A friend of God receives dominion over the works of God's hands and puts even death under his feet.

> PRAYER IS LIKE CHARGING YOUR SPIRITUAL BATTERY. WE ARE STRENGTHENED BY THE HOLY SPIRIT WHEN WE PRAY.

Prayer is like charging your spiritual battery. We are strengthened by the Holy Spirit when we pray. God's empowering presence speaks to us through His Holy Spirit. Just as Paul prayed in Ephesians 1:17, we pray for imparted wisdom and revelation so that we may know ("epignosis") God better.

The activity of the Spirit in bestowing divine power is in line with other New Testament verses where the Spirit and power are intimately linked. "But you will receive power when the Holy Spirit has come upon you" (Acts 1:8 ESV).

The Secret in the Secret Place

Jesus is the secret we find as we camp out in the secret place. Paul's deepest desire was to know Him deeply and to make Him known globally. This is why when Paul gave his resume to the church in Corinth, he said in our modern language, "I don't like to boast, but if I have to, I'd rather just boast on the cross, not necessarily in my infirmities. However, bringing this treasure to both the Jews and the Gentiles has caused me to have to endure so much hardship and persecution, a lot more than any man could possibly imagine. But I've done this as a good soldier in Christ. I continue to do this because of my great love for Him and His church. His love has consumed me. He's my everything. So, my greatest desire is to know Him!"

The secret of the secret place is that it is truly no place at all; He is a person. Even in Jesus' humanity, hours before He was going to walk through the greatest trial in human history, he told Peter, "Simon, Simon, behold, Satan demanded to have you, that he might sift you like wheat, but I have prayed for you that your faith may not fail. And when you have turned again, strengthen your brothers" (Luke 22:31-32 ESV). Moments before He faced ultimate pain, His thoughts were on us. How much more now in His divinity is He interceding for all of us? As the writer of Hebrews says, He lives to make intercession for us (Hebrews 7:25). "Therefore He is also able to save to the uttermost those who come to God through Him, since He always lives to make intercession for them" (NKJV). Jesus never hides; in fact, He longs to be found (Jeremiah 29:13). He is the priceless treasure we find when we search for Him in prayer.

Going Deep

George MacDonald said, "Never tell a child, 'you have a soul.' Teach him, 'you are a soul; you have a body.'"[7] There is an entity within all of us that has eternal existence. Our internal eternalness communes with the Alpha and the Omega. The intangible God speaks to the depths of us we cannot even see or comprehend. We serve the everlasting Father, and He desires that we focus and look at the health of our hearts.

Cultivating the inner life has its critics, but I think this is due to a lack of understanding. God wants to strengthen us on the inside to

---

7 George MacDonald, *Annals of a Quiet Neighborhood* (Leipzig: Tauchnitz, 1867).

move His strength into our hearts and souls. He does this in answer to prayer and by His Spirit.

Here is the great news: You are not alone in trying to be that prayer warrior for God, for Christ lives in you. "But if Christ is in you, although the body is dead because of sin, the Spirit is life because of righteousness" (Romans 8:10 ESV). When we received Jesus as our Savior, He came into our spirit. Now He's in us, so our "spirit is life" through His Spirit.

Because He lives in us, the Christian life is not trying to behave like Christ but allowing Him to live in and through us.

"I have been crucified with Christ. It is no longer I who live, but Christ who lives in me. And the life I now live in the flesh I live by faith in the Son of God, who loved me and gave himself for me" (Galatians 2:20 ESV). Because He lives in us, the Christian life is not trying to behave like Christ but allowing Him to live in and through us.

Dwell in His Presence

"He who dwells in the shelter of the Most High will abide in the shadow of the Almighty. I will say to the Lord, 'My refuge and my fortress, my God, in whom I trust'" (Psalms 91:1-2 ESV).

When you seek to cultivate a life of prayer, Psalm 91 will lift you into a realm where you will experience a miraculous accommodation in a shaded place with God. To dwell in the shadow of the Almighty is to live under the promise of God's protection. The Hebrew word "yasab" means "to dwell or abide" and is often used for being in God's presence.

The Hebrew "EL-ELYON," Most High God, is a name of God used in a number of Old Testament Scriptures, but it was mostly used in Genesis and the Psalms. This name stresses God's supreme power as the sovereign ruler of the world.

Shadow of the Almighty—The Bible contains rich imagery depicting the "shadow" of God and the people who dwell under it. The imagery tells us much about the character of God. It also opens links between ancient Israel and the people and events of the New Testament. What does it mean to live under the shadow? Isn't it a paradox to live in a shadow? Does not a shadow denote darkness, mystery, or fearfulness? Just the opposite. In the Bible, it's the best place to be, if it is God's shadow. As various Scripture texts reveal, the divine Shadow (Hebrew "tzel") is a poetic or metaphorical description of God's hand, presence, or Spirit.

The hymn writers and poets of Israel repeat the metaphor of being under the Shadow of God. More specifically, they seek to be in the shadow of His wings. God's wings cast shadows of protection over the psalmist.

You will find that pleasurable place, always thinking about God and trusting Him as the Almighty constant companion. The Lord stretches His "shadow" or "protective shade" over His people who set up camp in His presence.

When your life is surrounded by trouble and conflict, where can you flee to find a place of prayer? At some point in our lives, we have all felt fearful, exposed, and vulnerable. Nothing appears to hold together during those times, and we naturally feel isolated. Psalm 91:4 reminds us that we are not alone in our struggle. The psalmist employs two metaphors to demonstrate God's faithfulness. The first metaphor is animate, while the second is inanimate: "He will cover you with his pinions, and under his wings, you will find refuge; his faithfulness is a shield and buckler" (ESV). When you are in an inconceivable place with God, your spirit is in a better place, a place of refuge to pray. Psalm 17:8 adds more power to this verse: "Keep me as the apple of Your eye; Hide me under the shadow of Your wings" (NKJV).

"Shield and buckler" refers to God's truth. It is a new prayer that God would intervene and that He would go forth as a warrior against the enemies who seek to disrupt your place of prayer. Quenching fiery darts is the way to truth and is a most effective shield to diminish all swords of your enemy so that you can focus on prayer.

How to Pray the Scriptures

When you are prepared to pray but don't know what words to use, you can turn to the Scriptures, and God's Word will inspire you to pray. Your beginning point could be accurately interpreting your reading, and 2 Timothy 2:15 could be your first encouragement: "Study and do your best to present yourself to God approved, a workman [tested by trial] who has no reason to be ashamed, accurately handling and skillfully teaching the word of truth" (AMP). You will be inspired once you spend time studying this and other verses, and the words you read will enter into your heart; you will have more words to pray effectively.

You are not alone because the Holy Spirit often shows you what to pray. You can sense the Holy Spirit's work during your times of prayer. The Lord will often meet us when we close our eyes and fix our hearts on His, for this is where God speaks to us. But now we include the Holy Spirit as the most vital part of prayer.

"And I will pray the Father, and He will give you another Helper, that He may abide with you forever— the Spirit of truth, whom the world cannot receive because it neither sees Him nor knows Him; but you know Him, for He dwells with you and will be in you. I will not leave you orphans; I will come to you" (John 14:16-18 NKJV).

Likewise, the Spirit also helps in our weaknesses. "For we do not know what we should pray for as we ought, but the Spirit Himself makes intercession for us with groanings which cannot be uttered. Now, He who searches the hearts knows what the mind of the Spirit is because He makes intercession for the saints according to the will of God" (Romans 8:26-27 NKJV).

There are a variety of verses in the Bible that will inspire you to pray on different subjects. In Luke 18, Jesus used two parables to illustrate the power of prayer: the parable of the widow and the judge (verses 1-8), and the parable of the Pharisee and the tax collector (verses 9-14). As mentioned often in the Scriptures, Jesus used parables to make powerful points, inspiring thoughts about how to pray for certain circumstances.

In the first parable, Jesus focused on the point that we should "always pray and not give up" (Luke 18:1 NIV). He spoke to the hearers (us) through the life of the widow, by demonstrating that persistent asking of God through prayer has the power to bring forth change. Jesus indicated that God is the One who will "bring about justice for his chosen ones, who cry out to him day and night" (Luke 18:7 NIV).

The second parable teaches us to pray with humility. The Pharisee stood and prayed, "God, I thank You that I am not like other people," (Luke 18:11 NIV) and now we know how he acted in prayer. But here is how the tax collector prayed in verse 13: "But the tax collector stood at a distance. He would not even look up to heaven, but beat his breast and said, 'God, have mercy on me, a sinner'" (Luke 18:13 NIV). Humility is the pathway to God's throne room. It's the open door to the heart of God. God is not interested in your resume or all the great things you've done, nor in all the mistakes you've made. He desires your broken heart before Him. The psalmist says in Psalm 51:17, "The sacrifice you desire is a broken spirit. You will not reject a broken and repentant heart, O God" (NLT).

HUMILITY IS THE PATHWAY TO GOD'S THRONE ROOM. IT'S THE OPEN DOOR TO THE HEART OF GOD.

Our God Listens

God is beyond the mystery: "Clouds and darkness are round about him: righteousness and judgment are the habitation of his throne" (Psalms 97:2). David had cultivated a life with God where his prayers became a lifetime of dialogue with God.

In Psalm 5, David wept to the Lord, that He would hear and answer David's prayer, and he was certain that he was among the righteous and that his enemies (whom he referred to as the wicked) were among those whom God hated. Undoubtedly, David had forgotten all the times he had sinned and displeased God.

How often do we pray to God about the behaviors we want to be changed in others (who are hopefully listening)? Or do we ever give God suggestions for answering our prayers? To cultivate a life of prayer requires much time in the presence of God to understand what true prayer is, as indicated in the first three verses.

Psalm 5:1-3 is a presentation on prayer with God. “Give ear to my words, O Lord, Consider my meditation. Give heed to the voice of my cry, My King and my God, For to You I will pray. My voice You shall hear in the morning, O Lord; In the morning I will direct it to You, And I will look up” (NKJV).

David was a man of prayer, and his prayers were focused on God alone. “For to You will I pray.” Often, our prayers are filled with our essentials, requests, petitions, or intuitions alone, making us forget to focus on God and seek His face.

David began by calling on God to hear his prayer. You might imagine it being a smart move of the poet to get God’s attention because David longed for an audience with God. He repeated the same idea three times using the Hebrew parallelism method: “Give ear to my words.” “Give heed to the voice of my cry.” “My voice You shall hear in the morning.” The Book of Psalms is a collection of heart-cries. But they’re not just beautiful words; they point us to the Unseen God. We can know Him through the tear-stained weeping laments and the shouts of joy throughout its pages.

“Give ear to my words, O Lord, Consider my groaning”— First, you will notice that the word Lord is written in all capital letters. It is an indicator that the word being translated is not “Adonai” but “Yahweh,” the name God gave himself with Moses at the burning bush, “I AM.” Additionally, Hebrew “hă·gî” means a whisper, musing, murmuring. According to *Strong’s Concordance*, it also means meditation or musing. David thought deeply about his life, leading to sorrow and pain, and sought God for His restoration.

"Give heed to the voice of my cry, My King and my God"—David spoke of words, of crying for help. Considering that David was praying during the time of the incident with Absalom, this is understandable. He was facing a rebellious son, a rival to his throne and a person who intended to kill him if possible. But this is also a great way to grasp three aspects of prayer to God. First, when talking with God, there are words. David cried out because of his son. The Hebrew "shava" means to cry out for help.

"You will hear my voice in the morning"—Morning and evening times were sacred in the ancient world, as great men and women of God set aside time to pray. David lifted his voice to His Father in the morning, to honor Him at the beginning of his waking hours. This prepared his heart for the rest of his day. Giving God the firstfruits of our time in prayer declares to the world that we will keep our eyes fixed on Him alone, no matter what our day has in store for us. Jesus wanted to spend time with His Father in the early morning while it was still dark. Jesus got up, left the house, went to a secluded place, and prayed there (Mark 1:35).

Inspired to Pray Like Others

Many people have cultivated a life of prayer because the example of those who went before them taught them the price and power of prayer.

As Saint Teresa of Avila taught, "A beginner must look at himself as one setting out to make a garden for his Lord's pleasure, on most unfruitful soil which abounds in weeds. His majesty roots up the weeds and will put in good plants instead. Let us reckon that this is already done when the soul decides to practice prayer and has begun to do so."[8]

Brother Lawerence

Brother Lawrence was a monk from the Carmelite monastery in Paris in the 1600s. His book, *The Practice of the Presence of God,* has

---

8 St. Teresa and David Lewis, *The Life of St. Teresa of Avila* (Cosimo Classics, 2006).

sold an estimated 22 million copies in the English language alone and recounts his teachings on cultivating a life of prayer throughout his time in the Brotherhood.

He did not become famous overnight, which is a sign to everyone seeking to cultivate our prayer life. Brother Lawrence was born as Nicholas Herman, and he grew up very poor and served as a soldier to eat and keep himself alive. He was injured in war, and he then left the army to work as a footman, opening carriage doors for travelers and waiting tables.

As a young man, he decided to follow Jesus, and, at about forty, he became a lay brother with the Discalced (Barefoot) Carmelites. There he took the name Lawrence of the Resurrection. This poor man who seemed to have little influence would soon change the world through his testimony.

Lawrence's style of praying was simple, to pray without ceasing. He recounts in his book praying to God in every moment, taking every thought captive and redirecting it to the Father. Every action—working in the kitchen, running errands, listening to others—everything throughout the day was offered to God: "We ought not to be weary of doing little things for the love of God, who regards not the greatness of the work, but the love with which it is performed." Lawrence believed in doing all things unto the Lord.

He developed a joyful spirit and a reputation amongst those around him that spread to the community. He was sought out for his wisdom and spiritual guidance to leaders around the world, to teach them to pray in the presence of God.

As you read these last few sentences, my greatest prayer is that through the pages of this book, you've learned or been able to discover the power of cultivating a life of prayer. After all, it's the greatest desire in the heart of your Heavenly Father when He looks at you. He wants time with you. Nothing more, nothing less. His heart abounds with limitless treasures, and He longs to reveal these to you. May His holy love and His glorious presence overwhelm and consume you as you seek to spend time with Him. He's waiting and beckoning you to come if you will!

Now let us pray.

The Author

Bernie Moore was born and raised in New Orleans, Louisiana. He pursued his education at Louisiana State University and later attended Christ for the Nations for ministerial studies. He is an evangelist whose worldwide organization, Bernie Moore Ministries, has impacted more than thirty countries, and his leadership has reached over 2.2 million souls for Jesus. He is also connected with the Global Evangelist Alliance, a part of the Empowered21 Movement. Bernie and his wife, Nicole, have three children and live in Dallas, Texas.